GROWING IN STATURE

Helping Children and Families Grow in Faith

Adebola Adeoluwa-Boluwajaiye

writing as

Ms Debola

Growing in Stature

Helping Children and Families Grow in Faith

Copyright © 2025 by Adebola Adeoluwa-Boluwajaiye

All rights reserved.

No part of this publication may be reproduced, stored in a retrieval system, or transmitted in any form or by any means, electronic or mechanical, including photocopying or recording, without prior written permission of the publisher. Any attempts to do so will be deemed a direct violation of the copyright agreement.

All Scripture quotations are taken from the International Children's Bible unless otherwise stated.

ISBN: 978-1-9194115-0-7
ID Publishing House

Email: idpublishinghouse@outlook.com

This Book is a Gift

to

_____

From

_____

Date

_____

Acknowledgements

First, my deepest gratitude goes to God revealed to us in Jesus Christ. The Father of all creatives, the One whose breath birthed this book. Every page exists because He inspired it.

A heartfelt thank you to my husband, my Adeoluwa. In August 2024, you picked up my prayer journal, flipped through the pages and landed on the spot where I wrote "I sense the Lord leading me toward writing books." From that moment, you did not relent. Almost every day, you reminded me that if the Lord gave the word, He had also made the grace available, consistently encouraging me and finding ways to ease my schedule to make this journey lighter. Thank you for praying for me, believing in me, pushing me, and making this journey lighter. Your support, love, and leadership are gifts I treasure deeply.

To my head pastor, Apostle Bernard Antwi; thank you for shepherding me faithfully over the years. You are a blessing and a deep inspiration. Thank you for going through the final edits with me.

To Pastor Smith Agbonmwanre and Pastor Emmanuel Anefu; thank you for your teachings, your encouragement and your steady guidance.

To Pastor Nadia Osei; about two years ago you said something to me that fanned the flames of what I've been perceiving in my heart over the years. Thank you for speaking those words, because they strengthened the whispers in my heart.

To Mrs Isibhakhomen Angella Nwachukwu, thank you for your genuine mother's heart and for embracing me as your own. Thank you for graciously completing the first edits of this book and for encouraging me all the way.

And to Mr Farayola Gideon thank you. I deeply appreciate the creativity and excellence you poured into designing the internal pages of this book. You went above and beyond. Thank you for the professional wisdom you freely share with me time and time again.

The Heart Behind This Devotional

I believe God's word can be fluid.

(1 Peter 2:2 NKJV — "As newborn babes, desire the pure milk of the word, that you may grow thereby.")

Younger ones surprise us every day with how quickly they grasp songs, stories, languages, and even technology, often without being formally taught. In the same way, when we present God's truth to them early, clearly, and lovingly, their hearts absorb it deeply. They don't need us to water down the word, they just need us to bring it close to love it, understand it, and live by it.

Jesus didn't overlook younger ones. He welcomed them. In Matthew 18:2-3. He placed a little one right in the middle of His disciples and used that moment to show us that **a child's heart carries Heaven's posture.** And in Matthew 19:13-15, when His disciples tried to stop the children from coming to Him, Jesus insisted, "Let the little children come to Me, and do not hinder them; for the kingdom of heaven belongs to such as these."

He could have said, *"Children have no business here, are you trying to distract us from the serious issues we are tending to? They cannot understand kingdom matters yet. Bring them when they're older or oh, let us quickly attend to them so they can let us focus on serious matters."*

But He didn't. Instead, He met them and honoured their place in God's heart

Jesus wants to meet your younger ones while they are still young. The question is — will you bring them to Him?

There is no neutral ground when it comes to shaping a younger one's heart and worldview.

If parents and guardians do not intentionally disciple their younger ones with God's wisdom, the world will happily fill that gap without permission.

And when the world steps in, you cannot choose what it teaches or how it shapes them.

Through "Growing in Stature," I am gently guiding younger ones to see how God's word connects to their daily lives, helping them grow in wisdom, character, and faith. This devotional is more than a weekly reading plan; it is a tool for parents, carers, and teachers to help younger ones fall in love with God's word early and walk with Him for life.

Warmly,
Ms Debola.

Letter to Parents/Carers

Thank you for choosing to invest in the spiritual growth of your child. This devotional was written with you and your child in mind, to support you as you guide them on their journey with God. Please note that this is not a daily devotional. It is intentionally designed as a weekly one so children can stay with a topic long enough to understand it, practise it, and remember it. And while this a devotional primarily designed for children, the curriculum cuts across all ages; anyone, both young and old, who reads and applies it to their lives will be transformed.

Also, you will find more than 52 topics in this devotional. That is deliberate. There are 57 topics in total: **52 weekly devotionals for the calendar year, 1 end of the year review guide, and 4 special devotionals — When I Feel Sick, When I Have Bad Dreams, Birthday Blessing Devotional, Back to School.** These 4 special devotionals were created because every family navigates different seasons at different times, and it is helpful to have these topics available whenever they are needed.

The weekly structure prevents information overload for anyone using this devotional. Working with one theme repeatedly for a whole week builds repetition; and repetition builds familiarity.

Familiarity, when stewarded properly, leads to understanding. When younger ones hear the same truth repeatedly, it begins to sink deep into their hearts. So please do not be in a hurry. **Talk about each week's topic at least four or five times.** Read the Bible verses together. Discuss what they mean. Share simple examples from real life.

Each time you revisit a topic, something new stands out; a fresh thought, a deeper truth, or even a question from your child that opens a new door for learning. This is how younger ones grow in faith. Slow down with your child and enjoy the journey. And let every conversation, prayer and giggle become part of your child's foundation in Christ.

Warmly,
Ms Debola.

How to Use This Devotional

Growing in Stature is designed to help younger ones and the entire family learn God's word one week at a time. To give you and your child a few special moments each week with God. As you go through each topic together, you are bonding with your little one while helping them discover God's heart for them.

Here are some helpful ways to get the best out of each week:

1. Follow the week-by-week layout.
This devotional is carefully arranged to align with different seasons of the year, so following the week-by-week layout will help your younger one benefit the most. Even if you feel your child already knows a topic, let them go through it again. Repetition gives fresh understanding and helps truth settle deeper in their hearts. Read the title and Bible verses together. If your child can read, let them find the verses in their Bible themselves.

2. Read the devotional thought slowly.
Pause after each part and talk about what it means. Ask gentle questions like, "What do you think this means for us?" or "Have you felt this way before?"

3. Talk about the lesson.
Help your child connect the message to everyday life: school, home, friends, or family.

4. Pray together.
Encourage your child to pray in their own simple, sincere words. Avoid cutting them short or posturing them to pray a certain way; corrections can come later. For now, let them pray however it comes to them; refining will be done later.

5. Pray for your child.
Don't only pray with them, pray over them. Speak blessings, strength, wisdom, and God's peace over their lives. Let them see you pray for them. It teaches them that prayer is real, personal, and powerful, and it builds their confidence as they grow.

6. Help your child learn the 'Verse to Remember.'
Read it aloud, let them repeat it daily, and write it on a sticky note or card for their wall, mirror, lunchbox, or bedside. Seeing God's word often helps it settle in their hearts.

7. Do the activity.
Each week includes a simple challenge, drawing, or action to make learning fun and practical.

8. Repeat through the week.
Revisit each topic at least four or five times. Repetition helps younger ones remember, understand, and live out what they learn.

9. Bring it up during the day.
Gently remind them of the lessons and the verses during school drop-offs, mealtimes, playtime, or family time.

10. Use the special devotionals when needed.
The four special devotionals are for special moments: birthdays, new school year, when they feel sick, or when they have bad dreams. Show your child where these are so they can explore them on their own when needed.

There is no competition, the goal is to let younger ones know God for themselves. You are planting God's word in your child's heart, and God will use it to shape their future. As they see Him as real, kind, and close to them, little by little, truth grows, and that is how faith is built.

Warmly,
Ms Debola.

Letter to Young Ones

Dear Younger One,

I am so glad you are here. This devotional was created especially for you. God loves you deeply and wants to talk to you every day through His word. When you read the Bible, you are not reading ordinary words, you are reading God's heart for you.

You are growing, learning, and discovering new things every day. And just like your body grows strong when you eat good food, your spirit grows strong when you read God's word, pray, and listen to Him. Even if you think you are too young to know God and be involved with Him; Jesus does not think so. He loves younger ones and always draws them close.

When you read each week's devotional, take your time. Think about what the scripture is saying.

Talk to God about it. Ask questions from grown-ups. Write down what stands out to you. God is excited to teach you, guide you, and help you become everything He created you to be.

Most importantly, remember this:
You are known, you are loved, and you are important to God.

I am so proud of you for choosing to grow in faith.

Warmly,
Ms Debola.

TABLE OF CONTENTS

WEEK 1: GOD HAS A PLAN FOR ME..........................1

WEEK 2: GOD MADE ME SPECIAL..........................3

WEEK 3: GOD KNOWS ME..........................5

WEEK 4: GOD LOVES ME ALWAYS..........................7

WEEK 5: KNOWING JESUS FOR MYSELF (JESUS I WANT YOU TO SHOW YOURSELF TO ME)..........................9

WEEK 6: BEING KIND TO OTHERS..........................11

WEEK 7: SAYING THANK YOU..........................13

WEEK 8: CHOOSING GOOD FRIENDS..........................15

WEEK 9: OBEYING GOD AND MY PARENTS..........17

WEEK 10: TELLING THE TRUTH: BEING HONEST..........................19

WEEK 11: PRAYING EVERYDAY..........................21

WEEK 12: READING MY BIBLE..........................23

WEEK 13: LISTENING TO GOD..........................25

WEEK 14: EASTER: JESUS IS ALIVE..........................27

WEEK 15: TRUSTING JESUS..........................29

WEEK 16: FORGIVING OTHERS..........................31

WEEK 17:   BEING CONTENT: NOT COMPLAINING...33

WEEK 18:   LOVING MY FAMILY...................................35

WEEK 19:   SHARING THR GOOD NEWS....................37

WEEK 20:   SAYING NO TO TEMPTATION...................39

WEEK 21:   THINKING PURE THOUGHTS...................41

WEEK 22:   GOD MADE ME ON PURPOSE (GENDER IDENTITY)..43

WEEK 23:   WHEN I FEEL LEFT OUT...........................46

WEEK 24:   USING MY GIFTS FOR GOD......................48

WEEK 25:   USING MY MONEY GOD'S WAY...............51

WEEK 26:   PRAISING AND WORSHIPING GOD.........54

WEEK 27:   LEARNING TO BE PATIENT.....................56

WEEK 28:   CONTROLLING MY ANGER.....................58

WEEK 29:   CHOOSING JOY EVERYDAY.....................60

WEEK 30:   LEARNING TO SAY SORRY.......................62

WEEK 31:   BEING HUMBLE: NOT PROUD.................64

WEEK 32:   USING KIND WORDS...............................66

WEEK 33:   SPEAKING GOD'S WORD OVER MYSELF.68

- **WEEK 34:** SERVING GOD WITH A HAPPY HEART....70
- **WEEK 35:** DISOBEDIENCE AND IT'S CONSEQUENCES..72
- **WEEK 36:** FAITH MAKES ME STRONG.....................74
- **WEEK 37:** THE HOLYSPIRIT HELPS ME..................76
- **WEEK 38:** GOD HEARS ME WHEN I PRAY................78
- **WEEK 39:** RESPECTING TEACHERS AND LEADERS...80
- **WEEK 40:** CHOOSE GOD, NOT MAGIC (WITCHCRAFT & DARK POWERS).............................82
- **WEEK 41:** CHOOSING LIGHT, NOT DARKNESS........85
- **WEEK 42:** GUARDING WHAT I WATCH AND HEAR.87
- **WEEK 43:** WHEN I AM AFRAID................................89
- **WEEK 44:** WHEN I FEEL SAD.......................................91
- **WEEK 45:** OBEYING EVEN WHEN NO ONE IS WATCHING...93
- **WEEK 46:** WORKING HARD AND DOING MY BEST.95
- **WEEK 47:** AVOIDING GOSSIP......................................97
- **WEEK 48:** TRUSTING GOD'S PROMISES...................99
- **WEEK 49:** THANKFUL HEARTS PLEASE THE LORD..101

WEEK 50: JESUS CAME TO SAVE US..........................103

WEEK 51: GOD'S GREATEST GIFT.............................105

WEEK 52: GOD WITH US: EMMANUEL....................107

MY YEAR WITH GOD (REVIEW & GOAL SETTING)..109

BIRTHDAY DEVOTIONAL
(GOD MADE THIS DAY SPECIAL FOR YOU)...............112

WHEN I FEEL SICK..115

BAD DREAMS: PRAYERS FOR PEACEFUL SLEEP.....118

BACK TO SCHOOL: SHINE FOR JESUS......................120

CLOSING NOTE...124

GOD HAS A PLAN FOR ME

WEEK 1

BIBLE VERSE:

"You saw my body as it was formed. All the days planned for me were written in Your book before I was one day old." – Psalm 139:16.

DEVOTIONAL THOUGHT:
As we begin a new year, it is wonderful to remember that God already has a plan for you. Even before you were born, He planned every part of your life. Every year, every month, every day, God has written it all in His book. The Bible says, "Can't You see? I have carved your name on the palms of My hands!" (Isaiah 49:16a TPT). That means you are never forgotten.

God has already made provisions for you. He knows your needs even before you were born.

"Ms Debola, provisions? But I have things I want."

Yes, He has made provisions! God's plan includes everything you will ever need. You can talk to Him about anything, just like you ask mummy or daddy for water, food, or help. God listens carefully to every word you say, and He loves to take care of you.

LESSON / REFLECTION:
God has made good plans for me. He has provided everything I need. I will trust Him and talk to Him every day.

PRAYER:
Dear God, thank You for having a wonderful plan for my life. Thank You for thinking about me and providing everything I need. As I begin this new year, help me to walk in Your plan and remember that You care for me every day. In Jesus name I ask, Amen.

ACTIVITY / THOUGHT FOR THE WEEK:
Write or draw one thing you want God to do for you this year. Each day, thank Him for it and tell Him about it in your prayers.

VERSE TO REMEMBER:

God clothes the grass in the field like that. The grass is living today but tomorrow is thrown into the fire to be burned. So, you can be even more sure that God will clothe you. Don't have so little faith. Matthew 6:30.

GOD MADE ME SPECIAL

WEEK 2

BIBLE VERSE:

"You made my whole being. You formed me in my mother's body. I praise you because you made me in an amazing and wonderful way. What you have done is wonderful. I know this very well." – Psalm 139:13–14.

DEVOTIONAL THOUGHT:
When God made you, He smiled. He looked at your nose, your skin, your height, your hair, your head, your eyes, your smile, your voice, and your gifts and said, "You are very good!" (Genesis 1:31). You are not an accident. God took time to make you exactly how He wanted you to be.

Every part of you is special. Your laugh, your ideas, your kindness, and even the things that make you different are part of His plan. No one in the whole world can be you. God doesn't want you to try to be someone else He wants you to shine as who He made you to be.

Sometimes people may say hurtful things or make fun of others for being different, but remember, God never makes mistakes. When you look in the mirror, say, "God made me special, and I am loved." That is why you should never make fun of others because of how they look, talk, or act. Never join people who laugh at someone's body or face. When you do that, you are making fun of God's work, and that is not right. Each person is a masterpiece made by God.

LESSON / REFLECTION:
God made me in a special way. I am His wonderful creation, and so is everyone else. I will treat myself and others with love and respect.

PRAYER:
Dear God, thank You for making me special. Thank You for my nose, my skin, my height, my hair, my eyes, my smile, my voice, and every gift You gave me. Help me to see myself the way You see me and to love others too. In Jesus name I ask, Amen.

ACTIVITY / THOUGHT FOR THE WEEK:
Look in the mirror each morning and smile. Say, "God made me special!" Write or draw one thing that makes you unique and thank God for it.

If people make fun of you because of how you look, say to yourself, "It does not matter, I am God's image (Genesis 1:27), and God is perfect, so I am."

If you have ever laughed at or made fun of someone, go and apologise. Tell them you are sorry and ask God to help you be kind to everyone.

VERSE TO REMEMBER:

God looked at everything He had made, and it was very good. Genesis 1:31a.

_____
_____
_____
_____
_____
_____
_____

GOD KNOWS ME

WEEK 3

BIBLE VERSE:

"Lord, you have examined me and you know me. You know when I sit down and when I get up. You know my thoughts before I think them. You know where I go and where I lie down. You know everything I do. Lord, even before I say a word, you already know it." – Psalm 139:1–4

DEVOTIONAL THOUGHT:

God knows you more than anyone else in the whole world. He knows your name, your voice, your favourite food, the games you love to play, and the songs you like to sing. God knows how many hairs are on your head (Matthew 10:30). He even knows how you feel when you are happy or when you are sad.

Sometimes you might feel like no one understands how you feel, but Jesus does. Before you even say a word, He already knows what is in your heart. He watches over you when you sleep and when you wake up. He never forgets you, and He never gets tired of you.

"Ma, how can God know all of that?"

God made you! And because He loves you so much, He pays attention to every detail about your life. That is how special you are to Him.

LESSON / REFLECTION:

Jesus knows everything about me, and He still loves me. I can talk to Him about anything because He understands me completely.

PRAYER:
Dear Jesus, thank You for knowing me and understanding me. Thank You for caring about every part of my life. When I feel alone or misunderstood, help me to remember that You see me, You hear me, and You know me. In Jesus name I ask, Amen.

ACTIVITY / THOUGHT FOR THE WEEK:
Sit quietly for a few minutes and think about how big God is and how much He loves you. Then draw a picture of yourself and write, "God knows me, and He cares about me."

VERSE TO REMEMBER:

When five sparrows are sold, they cost only two pennies. But God does not forget any of them. Yes, God even knows how many hairs you have on your head. Don't be afraid, you are worth more than sparrows. Luke 12:6-7.

GOD LOVES ME ALWAYS
BIBLE VERSE:

WEEK 4

"We love because God first loved us." – 1 John 4:19.

DEVOTIONAL THOUGHT:
Before you ever said your first word or took your first step, God already loved you. His love came first. He loved you before you even knew about Him, and His love never ends.

God's love is not like human love that changes when people get angry or stop talking to each other. His love stays the same every day. When you do well, He loves you. When you make mistakes, He still loves you. God's love does not stop because it is not based on what you do, it is based on who He is.

Because God loves us first, He teaches us how to love others too. When you help your friends, share your toys, forgive someone, or give a hug, you are showing the kind of love that comes from God. Every time you love, you are showing that God's love is in you.

LESSON / REFLECTION:
God loved me first, and He will always love me. I will show His love to others just like He shows it to me.

PRAYER:
Dear God, thank You for loving me first. Thank You for showing me what true love means. Help me to love others the same way You love me with kindness, patience, and forgiveness. In Jesus name I ask, Amen.

ACTIVITY / THOUGHT FOR THE WEEK:
Cut out a paper heart and write inside it, "God loved me first." Decorate it and give it to someone this week as a reminder that God's love never ends.

VERSE TO REMEMBER:

The Father has loved us so much! He loved us so much that we are called the children of God. And we are really His children. But the people in the world do not understand that we are God's children, because they have not known him. 1 John 3:1.

KNOWING JESUS FOR MYSELF

WEEK 5

BIBLE VERSE: (Jesus, I Want You to Show Yourself to Me)

"You will search for me. And when you search for me with all your heart, you will find me!" – Jeremiah 29:13.

DEVOTIONAL THOUGHT:

Jesus is real, even though you cannot see Him with your eyes. You can feel Him in your heart, hear Him when you read His Word, and sense His peace when you pray. He is not just the God your parents talk about, He wants to be your God too.

You do not have to be a grown-up to know God. Jesus said, "Let the little children come to me. Don't stop them, because the kingdom of heaven belongs to people who are like these children." (Matthew 19:14) He loves it when children talk to Him, sing to Him, and spend time with Him.

When you talk to God in prayer, you can tell Him anything; what made you happy, what made you sad, what you need help with, and what you are thankful for.

"Ma, will God really answer me?"

Yes, He will. He may speak to your heart, give you peace, or help you understand something from the Bible. As you talk to Him every day, you'll begin to feel His love more. That is how God becomes real to you through a friendship that grows with time.

LESSON / REFLECTION:
God is not far away. He is close to me, and I can know Him for myself when I pray, listen, and read His Word.

PRAYER:
Dear God, I want to know You for myself. Please make Your presence real to me. Help me to hear You, feel Your peace, and follow You every day. I want to be close to You and love You more. In Jesus name I ask, Amen.

ACTIVITY / THOUGHT FOR THE WEEK:
Find a moment each day to talk to God. You can whisper, write, or sing your prayer.

When you want to sleep at night, ask God to make Himself real to you. Tell Him you want to see Him as you sleep and wake up feeling His love and peace. In the morning, write or draw what you felt or dreamed.

VERSE TO REMEMBER:

And this is eternal life: that men can know You, the only true God, and that men can know Jesus Christ, the One you sent. John 17:3.

_____

_____

_____

_____

_____

_____

_____

_____

_____

BEING KIND TO OTHERS

WEEK 6

BIBLE VERSE:

"Do not forget to do good to others. And share with them what you have. These are the sacrifices that please God." – Hebrews 13:16.

DEVOTIONAL THOUGHT:
Kindness is one of the best ways to show God's love. When you are kind to others, you are acting like Jesus. Being kind means helping, sharing, caring, and speaking gently. Every small act of kindness makes God happy.

Sometimes, being kind means sharing what you have your snacks, your toys, or your time. When you share, you are showing love and making someone else feel cared for. God sees every little thing you do, even when no one else does.

In Acts 9:36–41, there was a woman named Tabitha. She was always doing good and helping the poor. One day, Tabitha became very sick and died, and the people who loved her were very sad. They sent two men to call Peter, one of Jesus' disciples, to come quickly. Peter came, prayed, and God brought Tabitha back to life. Everyone was filled with joy and many believed in Jesus because of this.

"Ma, what if someone is unkind to me?"

You can still be kind by praying for them. You don't have to fight or say bad words. You can excuse yourself for a moment, remove yourself from the environment, or walk away quietly.

Choosing peace does not make you weak; it shows that God's kindness lives in your heart. Ask God to help you forgive and show love, just like Jesus did.

LESSON / REFLECTION:
Kindness is more than words. It means helping, sharing, and forgiving others because that's what God does for me.

PRAYER:
Dear God, thank You for being kind to me and giving me good things every day. Help me to be kind to others, to share what I have, and to forgive quickly. Let my kindness show others how much You love them. In Jesus name I ask, Amen.

ACTIVITY / THOUGHT FOR THE WEEK:
Think of one person you can be kind to this week. You can share your snack, give a helping hand, or write them a kind note. Each time you do something kind, say, "I am showing God's love."

> **VERSE TO REMEMBER:**
>
> *Then a Samaritan traveling down the road came to where the hurt man was lying. He saw the man and felt very sorry for him. Luke 10:33.*

SAYING THANK YOU

WEEK 7

BIBLE VERSE:

"Give thanks to the Lord, because He is good. His love continues forever." – Psalm 107:1.

DEVOTIONAL THOUGHT:
"Thank you" are two small words that make a big difference. When you say thank you, you are showing that you notice kindness and that you have a thankful heart. God loves it when we say thank you not just to people, but to Him too.

Every new day, every meal, every smile, and even the air we breathe are gifts from God. Sometimes we forget to say thank you because we are busy or we think small things do not matter, but nothing is too small to thank God for.

"Do I have to say thank you all the time?"

Yes, because a thankful heart is a happy heart. When you thank God, you remind yourself of how good He is. And when you thank people, you show them love and respect. Gratitude makes everyone around you feel joyful.

LESSON / REFLECTION:
God loves a thankful heart. I will remember to say thank you to God and to people every day.

PRAYER:

Dear God, thank You for everything You have given me, my family, my friends, my food, and my life. Help me not to forget Your goodness. Teach me to always say thank You and to mean it from my heart. In Jesus name I ask, Amen.

ACTIVITY / THOUGHT FOR THE WEEK:

Each day, think of three things you are thankful for and write or draw them. At the end of the week, look at your list and tell God, "Thank You for everything You've done!" Remember to also say thank you to someone who helped you or showed you kindness this week.

VERSE TO REMEMBER:

When one of them saw that he was healed, he went back to Jesus. He praised God in a loud voice. Then he bowed down at Jesus' feet and thanked Him. (This man was a Samaritan.) Jesus asked, "Ten men were healed, where are the nine? Luke 17: 15-17.

_____

_____

_____

_____

_____

_____

_____

_____

_____

_____

_____

_____

CHOOSING GOOD FRIENDS

WEEK 8

BIBLE VERSE:

"Do not be fooled. 'Bad friends will ruin good habits.'" – 1 Corinthians 15:33.

DEVOTIONAL THOUGHT:
Friends can make a big difference in your life. The people you spend time with can help you grow closer to God, His plans for you, and your family. That is why it is important to choose your friends wisely.

Good friends will encourage you to do the right thing. They will remind you to pray, to be kind, to obey your parents, to study, and to be hardworking. But bad friends may try to make you lie, fight, or disobey. When you choose friends who love God, they will help you become the best version of yourself.

"Ma, what if my friend does bad things?"

You should still be nice to them but be careful not to copy their wrong choices. If they keep doing things that displease God, you should step away from them and move closer to friends who love God and help you do what is right. You can pray for them and ask God to help them change, but your heart must stay close to those who draw you nearer to Him.

LESSON / REFLECTION:
Good friends bring me closer to God and help me live in His plan for

my life. I will choose my friends wisely and be a good influence on others.

PRAYER:
Dear God, thank You for the friends in my life. Please help me to choose good friends who love You, support my family, and help me grow in faith. Give me the courage to walk away from anyone who leads me into trouble. In Jesus name I ask, Amen.

ACTIVITY / THOUGHT FOR THE WEEK:
With the help of your parent or guardian, write or draw three things that make a good friend and three things that make a bad friend. Ask God to help you be the kind of friend that leads others to do good and grow closer to Him.

VERSE TO REMEMBER:

When David finished talking with Saul, Jonathan felt very close to David. He loved David as much as he loved himself. 1 Samuel 18:1.

OBEYING GOD AND MY PARENTS WEEK 9
BIBLE VERSE:

"Honour your father and your mother, that your days may be long in the land which your LORD your God is giving you." – Exodus 20:12 NKJV.

DEVOTIONAL THOUGHT:
Obedience means doing what you are asked to do with a good attitude. God loves it when children obey their parents, teachers, and elders because it shows that they respect and trust Him. When you obey, you make God happy and bring peace into your home.

Sometimes, obeying can be hard especially when you want to do something else. But even Jesus obeyed His parents when He was a child. The Bible says He listened to them and grew in wisdom and favour. When you obey, you are following Jesus' example.

"Ma, what if I don't feel like obeying?"

You can ask God to help you. Obedience becomes easier when you remember that God sees your heart. Every time you choose to obey, you are showing your love for God and honouring your parents.

"Ms Debola, what if my teacher or an elderly person asks me to do something that is not godly?"

That happens sometimes. You should politely explain why you cannot obey that instruction and tell your parents, guardian, or pastor about it. God wants you to obey those in authority, but never to do anything

that goes against His Word. True obedience always pleases God first.

LESSON / REFLECTION:
Obedience makes God happy. When I obey my parents and those who care for me, I am also obeying God.

PRAYER:
Dear God, thank You for my parents and everyone who guides me. Help me to listen and obey quickly, with a joyful heart. Teach me to remember that obedience is one way I can show my love for You. In Jesus name I ask, Amen.

ACTIVITY / THOUGHT FOR THE WEEK:
This week, look for ways to obey at home maybe cleaning up, helping with chores, or listening the first time you are called.

With the help of your parent or guardian, write or draw one thing you obeyed about each day and thank God for helping you do it.

> **VERSE TO REMEMBER:**
>
> *But Samuel answered, "What pleases the Lord more: burnt offerings and sacrifices or obedience? It is better to obey God than to offer a sacrifice. It is better to listen to God than to offer the fat of male sheep." 1 Samuel 15:22.*

_____

_____

_____

_____

_____

TELLING THE TRUTH: BEING HONEST — WEEK 10

BIBLE VERSE:

"Don't use your mouth to tell lies. Don't ever say things that are not true." – Proverbs 4:24.

DEVOTIONAL THOUGHT:
Telling the truth means saying what really happened and not hiding or changing the story. Jesus wants us to always be honest because He is a God of truth. When you tell the truth, people can trust you, and you make Jesus proud.

Sometimes, it can be hard to tell the truth because you are afraid of getting into trouble. But lying only makes things worse. Even when it feels difficult, Jesus wants you to be brave and truthful. He will help you say the truth with kindness.

"Ma, what if I already told a lie?"

You can tell the truth now. Say sorry to Jesus and to the person you lied to. Jesus forgives those who come to Him with a sincere heart. When you tell the truth, you show that Jesus' light is shining inside you.

LESSON / REFLECTION:
Jesus is pleased when I tell the truth. I will always speak the truth and be honest, even when it's hard.

Help me always tell the truth.

PRAYER:
Dear Jesus, thank You for teaching me to tell the truth. Please help me to always be honest in my words and actions. Forgive me for times I have not told the truth and help me to be trustworthy and brave. In Jesus name I ask, Amen.

ACTIVITY / THOUGHT FOR THE WEEK:
With the help of your parent or guardian, read a Bible story about honesty, such as the story of Ananias and Sapphira (Acts 5:1–11). Talk about what happened and why it's important to always tell the truth. Then write or draw one way you can be honest this week

> **VERSE TO REMEMBER:**
>
> *Peter said, "Ananias, why did you let satan rule your heart? You lied to the Holy Spirit. Why did you keep part of the money you received for the land for yourself?" The Acts 5:3*

PRAYING EVERY DAY
(TALKING TO JESUS)

WEEK 11

BIBLE VERSE:

"Never stop praying." – 1 Thessalonians 5:17.

DEVOTIONAL THOUGHT:
Prayer is how we talk to Jesus. You don't need big words or special clothes to pray; you can pray anywhere, anytime. Jesus loves hearing your voice. When you pray, you are not just talking to the air; you are talking to your heavenly Father who listens carefully to every word you say.

You should pray when you wake up, before you eat, before getting into the car, bus, or train, when you get to school, and when you get home. You should pray before you sleep at night and thank Jesus for keeping you safe all day.

Pray when you feel sick and pray when your friends or parents feel sick too. As you visit the doctor, pray that Jesus will help the doctor to help you well. You can also pray when you are happy, sad, scared, or thankful, Jesus wants to be part of everything you do.

"Ma, does Jesus really hear me?"

Yes, He does. Jesus hears even your quietest prayers. Sometimes He answers right away, and sometimes He wants you to wait and trust Him. But He always listens and always cares.

LESSON / REFLECTION:
Prayer is my way to talk to Jesus. I will pray every day and trust that He hears me.

PRAYER:
Dear Jesus, thank You for always listening to me. Please help me to pray every day, not just when I need something. Teach me to talk to You as my friend and to listen when You speak to my heart. In Jesus name I ask, Amen.

ACTIVITY / THOUGHT FOR THE WEEK:
Make a prayer list with the help of your parent or guardian. Write or draw three things you want to thank God for, three things you want to ask God for, and three people you want to pray for. Pray about them every day this week.

VERSE TO REMEMBER:
Early next morning, Jesus woke and left the house while it was still dark. He went to a place to be alone and pray. Mark 1:35.

READING MY BIBLE

WEEK 12

BIBLE VERSE:

"Your word is like a lamp for my feet, a light for my way." – Psalm 119:105.

DEVOTIONAL THOUGHT:
The Bible is not just a book; it is God's word to you. It teaches you Who God is, His ways and how much He loves you. The Bible tells you about people who walked with God, about those who disobeyed Him, the things God did, His promises for you, and His instructions for your life.

When you read your Bible, you are listening to God speak to your heart. You should read your Bible every day, even if it is just one verse. You can read it in the morning, before bed, or during quiet time. God's Word gives you wisdom, comfort, and strength to do the right thing.

"Ms Debola, what if I don't understand what I read?"

That's okay and very normal. You can ask your parents, teacher, or pastor to explain it to you. You can also ask the Holy Spirit to help you understand. The more you read, the more you will learn and grow, so don't stop reading the bible because you do not understand it yet.

LESSON / REFLECTION:
The Bible is God's word to me. I will read it every day and obey what it says.

PRAYER:
Dear God, thank You for giving me Your word. Please help me to love reading my Bible and to understand what You are teaching me. Let Your word guide my thoughts and help me make good choices. In Jesus name I ask, Amen.

ACTIVITY / THOUGHT FOR THE WEEK:
With the help of your parent or guardian, choose a Bible verse to read every day this week. After reading, say what you learned or draw a small picture about it. You can also write one verse you love and put it by your bed to remember it.

> **VERSE TO REMEMBER:**
>
> *Always remember what is written in the Book of the Teachings. Study it day and night. Then you will be sure to obey everything that is written there. If you do this, you will be wise and successful in everything. Joshua 1:8.*

_____

_____

_____

_____

_____

_____

_____

_____

LISTENING TO GOD
BIBLE VERSE:

WEEK 13

"My sheep listen to my voice. I know them, and they follow me."
– John 10:27

DEVOTIONAL THOUGHT:
"Ms Debola, but Jesus was talking about sheep! I am not a sheep!"

Yes, you are human, but Jesus was speaking in a special way to help us understand something important. He was comparing us to sheep not because we have wool or walk on four legs but because sheep listen to their shepherd's voice and follow only him. Jesus is our Shepherd, and we are His children. Just like sheep know the voice of their shepherd, we can learn to know and follow the voice of Jesus.

Listening to God means paying attention to what He says through the Bible, through the Holy Spirit, and sometimes through your parents, teachers, or pastors. Jesus still speaks today; you just need to learn to be quiet enough to hear Him.

When you read your Bible, pray, or worship, God can speak to your heart. He might remind you of something you should do or gently tell you not to do something wrong. His voice will never tell you to hurt anyone or disobey His Word.

"Ma, how do I know it's Jesus speaking?"

You can know it's Jesus when what you hear or feel agrees with His Word and brings peace to your heart. Jesus' voice is loving, kind, and gentle. He never shouts in anger. The more time you spend with Him, the easier it becomes to know His voice. Listening to Jesus also means obeying what He says. When you listen and obey, you show that you trust Him.

LESSON / REFLECTION:
God speaks to me through His word and in my heart. I will listen carefully and obey what He says.

PRAYER:
Dear God, thank You for always speaking to me. Please help me to listen to Your voice and obey quickly when You speak. Teach me to hear You clearly and follow You every day. In Jesus name I ask, Amen.

ACTIVITY / THOUGHT FOR THE WEEK:
Find a quiet time each day to pray and be still for a few minutes. Ask God to speak to your heart. Then write or draw what you feel He is teaching you.

VERSE TO REMEMBER:

"Samuel said, speak, Lord. I am your servant, and I am listening." – 1 Samuel 3:10b.

_____
_____
_____
_____
_____
_____

EASTER: JESUS IS ALIVE

WEEK 14

BIBLE VERSE:

"But He is not here. He has risen from death as He said He would! Come and see the place where His body was." – Matthew 28:6

DEVOTIONAL THOUGHT:
Early Sunday morning, following the crucifixion and burial of Jesus; some women went to visit the place where Jesus was buried. They were sad because Jesus had died on the cross. But when they got there, something wonderful had happened, the big stone had been rolled away, and the tomb was empty!

An angel told them, "He is not here. He has risen just as He said!" Jesus had come back to life, just like He promised. That means He has power over death, sin, and everything that tries to make us afraid.

Ms Debola, why did Jesus have to die?

Jesus died to take away our sins so that we can be close to God again. But the story didn't end there He came back to life to show that His power is greater than anything in the world. Because Jesus is alive, we can talk to Him anytime. We can have peace, joy, and hope every single day.

LESSON / REFLECTION:
Jesus is alive; someday, we shall be, and reign with Him.

Jesus is alive, and because He lives, I can live with joy and hope every day.

PRAYER:
Dear Jesus, thank You for dying for my sins and rising again. Thank You for showing me that nothing is too hard for You. Help me to remember that You are alive in me and with me always. In Jesus name I ask, Amen.

ACTIVITY / THOUGHT FOR THE WEEK:
Draw or colour a picture of an empty tomb with the words "Jesus Is Alive!" Each time you see it, say aloud, "Jesus is alive, and He lives in me!"

VERSE TO REMEMBER:

"In a little while the world will not see me anymore, but you will see me. Because I live, you will live, too." – John 14:19.

_____
_____
_____
_____
_____
_____
_____
_____
_____
_____

TRUSTING JESUS

WEEK 15

BIBLE VERSE:

"You, Lord, give true peace. You give peace to those who depend on you. You give peace to those who trust you. So, trust the Lord always. Trust the Lord because he is our Rock forever." – Isaiah 26:3–4.

DEVOTIONAL THOUGHT:
When you trust Jesus, He gives you peace. Peace is your right as a child of God; Jesus made the provision. "I leave you my peace. My peace I give you. I do not give it to you as the world does. So, don't let your hearts be troubled. Don't be afraid. John 14:27".

That means you can feel calm and safe inside, even when things around you seem scary or confusing. God wants you to depend on Him every day because He never changes, He is your rock forever.

Sometimes, things might not go the way you want. Maybe you studied hard for a test but didn't do well, or you felt nervous about something at school. Maybe your sick friend whom you hoped would get well didn't get well. In those moments, remember that God is with you and that He gives peace to those who trust Him.

"Ma, what if I get scared?"

It is okay to get scared. Grown-ups get scared too, but we don't let it stop us. So, when you get scared, you should tell Jesus about it. He will calm your heart and remind you that He is right beside you. Jesus' peace is like a warm hug that makes your heart feel safe again.

When you trust Jesus, you don't have to worry. You can rest knowing that He is in control and that His plan for your life is good.

LESSON / REFLECTION:
When I trust Jesus, He gives me peace. I will depend on Him and remember that He is my rock forever.

PRAYER:
Dear Jesus, thank You for being my rock and my peace. Please help me to trust You every day. When I start to feel afraid or unsure, remind me that You are with me and that I can depend on You always. In Jesus name I ask, Amen.

ACTIVITY / THOUGHT FOR THE WEEK:
With the help of your parent or guardian, draw a big rock and write inside it the words "Jesus is my Rock." Then write or draw one thing that worries you and pray, "Jesus, I trust You to give me peace about this."

VERSE TO REMEMBER:
Trust the Lord with all your heart. Don't depend on your own understanding. Remember the Lord in everything you do. And He will give you success. Proverbs 3:5-6.

_____
_____
_____
_____
_____
_____
_____

FORGIVING OTHERS

WEEK 16

BIBLE VERSE:

"Yes, if you forgive others for the things they do wrong, then your Father in heaven will also forgive you for the things you do wrong." – Matthew 6:14.

DEVOTIONAL THOUGHT:
Forgiving others means letting go of the hurt someone caused you and choosing not to stay angry. God wants us to forgive because He forgives us too. When we forgive, our hearts become lighter, and we make room for peace and joy.

Sometimes, people may say mean things or hurt our feelings. Forgiving them doesn't mean what they did was okay; it means you are choosing peace over anger. When Jesus was on the cross, He forgave the people who hurt Him. That shows how big His love is.

"Ma, what if it still hurts?"

You can forgive and still feel sad for a while. You can tell God how you feel and ask Him to help you feel better. You shouldn't hold back forgiveness because you're still hurt. Jesus was still on the cross, in pain, when He forgave those who hurt Him. Forgiveness doesn't wait for the pain to go away it helps the pain heal faster.

LESSON / REFLECTION:
I will forgive others because God forgives me. Forgiveness brings peace to my heart.

PRAYER:
Dear God, thank You for forgiving me every day. Please help me to forgive others, even when it's hard. Take away anger or hurt from my heart and fill me with Your peace and love. In Jesus name I ask, Amen.

ACTIVITY / THOUGHT FOR THE WEEK:
With the help of your parent or guardian, write or draw one person you need to forgive. Pray for them and ask God to bless them. If you can, tell them "I forgive you." If not, say it quietly to God. Forgive from your heart and feel His peace.

VERSE TO REMEMBER:

But I tell you, love your enemies. Pray for those who hurt you. Matthew 5:44.

_____
_____
_____
_____
_____
_____
_____
_____
_____
_____
_____
_____
_____
_____

BEING CONTENT: NOT COMPLAINING — WEEK 17

BIBLE VERSE:

"And be satisfied with what you have. God has said, 'I will never leave you; I will never abandon you.'" – Hebrews 13:5b.

DEVOTIONAL THOUGHT:

Being content means being happy and thankful for what you have instead of complaining about what you don't have. God wants us to learn to say, "thank You" instead of "why don't I have this?" because He has already given us so much.

Being content does not mean you will not desire better or try to be better. It simply means being grateful for what you have and where you are, while working hard and trusting God for something greater. When you are content, you are not sad about what you don't have, you are thankful for what you do have.

Complaining, on the other hand, means focusing on what is missing and speaking unhappy or unkind words because of it. When we complain, we forget that God has been good to us. Complaining takes away our joy, but gratitude fills our hearts with peace.

"Ms Debola, what if I really want something?"

It's okay to want things, but don't let it take away your joy. You can tell God what you want and trust Him to give it to you at the right time or to give you something even better.

Remember, being content shows that you trust God's plan and that you are grateful for what He has already done.

LESSON / REFLECTION:
Being content means trusting God's timing while being thankful for what I have. Complaining steals my joy, but gratitude keeps my heart happy.

PRAYER:
Dear God, thank You for everything You have given me. Please help me to be content and not complain. Teach me to be thankful where I am, while I work and trust You for better things ahead. In Jesus name I ask, Amen.

ACTIVITY / THOUGHT FOR THE WEEK:
With the help of your parent or guardian, write or draw five things you are thankful for today. Each time you feel like complaining this week, look at your list and thank God for those things instead.

VERSE TO REMEMBER:

"The fear of the Lord leads to life, and he who has it will abide in satisfaction; He will not be visited with evil." – Proverbs 19:23 NKJV

_____
_____
_____
_____
_____
_____
_____
_____

LOVING MY FAMILY

WEEK 18

BIBLE VERSE:

"It is good and pleasant when God's people live together in peace!" – Psalm 133:1.

DEVOTIONAL THOUGHT:

Family is one of God's greatest gifts. He put you in your family on purpose to love, learn, and grow together. Loving your family means helping one another, speaking kindly, sharing, forgiving, and praying for one another.

You should talk to your siblings kindly even when they upset you, help when you see them struggling, and forgive them quickly. That is one of the best ways to show that God's love lives in your heart. Sometimes, family members may get on your nerves or make you upset. But loving your family means choosing patience and kindness even when you don't feel like it. God wants your home to be filled with love and peace.

"Ma, what if someone in my family makes me angry or sad?"

You should take a deep breath, talk to God about it, and choose not to say hurtful things. You can tell your parent or guardian how you feel but still show respect. Love means saying "I'm sorry" when you're wrong and forgiving when others hurt you. That's how peace stays in the family. When you love your family, you make God happy because you are showing His love in your home. Remember, family is not perfect, but love makes it strong.

LESSON / REFLECTION:
God gave me my family to love and care for. I will be kind, patient, and forgiving at home.

PRAYER:
Dear God, thank You for my family. Please help me to love them the way You want me to; with patience, kindness, and forgiveness. Let peace and joy fill our home every day. In Jesus name I ask, Amen.

ACTIVITY / THOUGHT FOR THE WEEK:
With the help of your parent or guardian, do something nice for your family this week. You can help with chores, write a thank-you note, pray for each person by name, or you can do all! Talk about how love makes your family stronger.

> **VERSE TO REMEMBER:**
>
> *"Love each other like brothers and sisters. Give your brothers and sisters more honour than you want for yourselves." – Romans 12:10*

_____
_____
_____
_____
_____
_____
_____
_____
_____
_____
_____

SHARING THE GOOD NEWS
(TELLING OTHERS ABOUT JESUS)

WEEK 19

BIBLE VERSE:

"So go and make followers of all people in the world. Baptize them in the name of the Father and of the Son and of the Holy Spirit." – Matthew 28:19.

DEVOTIONAL THOUGHT:
The Good News is that Jesus loves everyone, forgives sins, and wants us to live with Him forever. But not just us, He wants the whole world to know about Him and accept Him as their Lord and Saviour. God wants every child, every family, and every nation to know that Jesus saves.

You don't need to stand on a big stage or use a microphone to tell people about Jesus. You can start right where you are at school, in your home, or with your friends.

"Ms Debola, what if I feel shy?"

It's okay to feel shy, but you can start small. Here's how you can share Jesus step by step:
- Pray for them: Tell Jesus about your friends or family who don't know Him yet. Ask Him every day to help them know His love.
- Show them kindness: Smile, share, and help them. Your kindness shows them Jesus' heart.
- Talk about what Jesus has done for you and people close to you: maybe how healed you, or how he helped your parents or sibling.

- Keep praying: Don't stop praying for them. God listens every time you pray.
- Invite them to church or Sunday school: You can say, "Would you like to come to church with me?" or "We're learning about Jesus and it's really fun!"

Every time you show love, you are sharing Jesus. You may not see it right away, but God uses your kindness to touch their hearts.

LESSON / REFLECTION:
I can share Jesus' love by praying, helping, and speaking kindly. God can use me to bring others to Him.

PRAYER:
Dear God, thank You for sending Jesus to save me. Please help me to be brave and loving when I tell others about You. Use my words and my actions to show Your love to my friends and family. In Jesus name I ask, Amen.

ACTIVITY / THOUGHT FOR THE WEEK:
Make a list of two or three people you want to tell about Jesus. Pray for them every day this week and look for ways to be kind to them.

> **VERSE TO REMEMBER:**
> "Sing to the Lord and praise His name. Every day tell how He saves us. Tell the nations of His glory. Tell all peoples the miracles He does." – Psalm 96:2–3.

_____

_____

_____

_____

SAYING NO TO TEMPTATION
(DOING WHAT IS RIGHT)

WEEK 20

BIBLE VERSE:

"The only temptations that you have are the temptations that all people have. But you can trust God. He will not let you be tempted than you can stand. But when you are tempted, God will also give you a way to escape that temptation. Then you will be able to stand it." – 1 Corinthians 10:13

DEVOTIONAL THOUGHT:
Temptation means wanting to do something you know is wrong. It could be taking what doesn't belong to you, telling a lie, being rude, or not obeying your parents. Sometimes, temptation can also mean believing things that are not true about God or yourself; things that do not agree with what the Bible says.

Everyone faces temptation; even Jesus was tempted but He didn't sin. He said no to the devil by speaking God's Word. That means we can also use God's Word to stay strong and do what is right.

When you are tempted, it might feel like a small voice is saying, "No one will know." But remember, God always sees and He can help you make the right choice. You are stronger than temptation when you ask God for help.

"Ma, what should I do when I feel tempted?"

You should stop and think before you act! Ask yourself, "Would this make God happy?" If the answer is no, then don't do it.

You can also pray and say, "God, please help me do what is right."

God promises to always give you a way out, a way to say no and walk away. When you say no to temptation, you make God proud and keep your heart clean.

LESSON / REFLECTION:
I can say no to wrong choices and wrong thoughts because God gives me strength to do what is right.

PRAYER:
Dear God, thank You for helping me to do what is right. Please give me the strength to say no to anything that does not please You. Help me to remember Your Word when I feel tempted or confused. In Jesus name I ask, Amen.

ACTIVITY / THOUGHT FOR THE WEEK:
With the help of your parent or guardian, talk about situations where you might be tempted like cheating, lying, being unkind, or believing something wrong about yourself or God. Write or draw what you can do instead when those moments come.

> **VERSE TO REMEMBER:**
>
> *"And stay away from everything that is evil." – 1 Thessalonians 5:22*

_____
_____
_____
_____
_____
_____
_____

THINKING PURE THOUGHTS

WEEK 21

BIBLE VERSE:

"Be very careful about what you think. Your thoughts run your life– Proverbs 4:23.

DEVOTIONAL THOUGHT:

Your thoughts are like seeds, whatever you plant in your mind will grow in your heart. If you think about good things, love, peace, and kindness will grow. But if you keep thinking about bad, scary, or wrong things, they can fill your heart with fear, anger, or sadness.

That's why God tells us to think about what is good, true, and pure. When you fill your mind with Bible verses, songs about Jesus, and thoughts about God's goodness, you feel happy and peaceful inside.

Ms Debola, can I control what I think about?

Yes, you can! When a bad or wrong thought comes to your mind, you should not keep it there. You should remove it and say something godly immediately. You can sing, pray, or say a memory verse to help your mind stay full of God's Word.

God made your mind strong, and He wants you to use it to think about things that bring light, not darkness. The more you think about good things, the more like Jesus you become.

LESSON / REFLECTION:
I will fill my mind with good, godly thoughts and not let bad thoughts stay in my heart.

PRAYER:
Dear God, thank You for giving me a sound and peaceful mind. Help me to think good thoughts that please You. When bad thoughts come, remind me of Your word and help me to choose what is true and pure. In Jesus name I ask, In Jesus name I ask, Amen.

ACTIVITY / THOUGHT FOR THE WEEK:
Write or draw three good thoughts that you want to think about this week. Say them out loud every morning and thank God for giving you a peaceful mind.

VERSE TO REMEMBER:

"Those who are pure in their thinking are happy. They will be with God." – Matthew 5:8.

_____
_____
_____
_____
_____
_____
_____
_____
_____
_____

GOD MADE ME ON PURPOSE
(GENDER IDENTITY)

WEEK 22

BIBLE VERSE:

"So, God created human beings in His own image. In the image of God, He created them. He created them male and female." – Genesis 1:27.

DEVOTIONAL THOUGHT:
God never makes mistakes. When He created you, He already decided who you would be; a boy or a girl, and that is the gender you were born with! The body you were born in is His exact design for you. He looked at you and said, "Very good!" (Genesis 1:31).

Your gender is part of God's wonderful plan for you. It is not something to be confused about or ashamed of, you are at your best in the body God assigned to you. He gave you everything you need to be exactly who He made you to be. God knew you even before your mum carried you in her belly (Psalms 139:15), and He designed your life, your friends, and your future with your identity in mind.

Ms Debola, what if someone says I was born in the wrong body?

That's not true, that is a misunderstanding. Confusion sometimes happens due to different reasons; and when that happens, it is the mind that needs love, truth, support, and clarity, **not the body that needs changing**. God created the body and identity of every child with care and purpose to match everything else about them.

Ma, what if I feel like I should act like and become the other gender?

We are not led by our feelings, because not all feelings are true. Just because you feel like you don't like your family or friends does not mean you don't like them, you do like them, you only feel like you do not like them. Acting on that feeling to hurt them will only leave a forever scar that no one likes. So having certain thoughts or feelings does not make them right or godly.

We will soon be learning about the Holy Spirit. What makes any thought godly is that it agrees with the word of God. And God's word says, "You are fearfully and wonderfully made." (Psalm 139:14)

So, if at all, or whenever this feeling/thought of wanting to be like the other gender comes; remember, it is not true and should not be followed. Then, say over yourself: **"Lord Jesus, clean and rule over my heart and mind", "I have the mind of Christ, so my thoughts are pure", God made me perfectly, and He never gets it wrong."**

Some people have tried to change how God made them, but it never brought them true peace or happiness. They later realised that real joy only comes from accepting who God made them to be.

When you thank God for who you are, you are agreeing with Him. Boys and girls are both precious to God; different, but equal in His love.

LESSON / REFLECTION:
God made me a (mention your gender) on purpose, and His plan for me is perfect.

PRAYER:
Dear God, thank You for making me who I am, thank You for my body, my mind, and my heart.

Help me to love who You made me to be and to never be confused or ashamed of it. In Jesus name I ask, Amen.

ACTIVITY / THOUGHT FOR THE WEEK:
Look in the mirror and say, "God made me on purpose, and I am very good!"

Write or draw three things you love about how God made you.

VERSE TO REMEMBER:

"I praise You because You made me in an amazing and wonderful way. What You have done is wonderful. I know this very well. – Psalm 139:14.

_____
_____
_____
_____
_____
_____
_____
_____
_____
_____
_____
_____
_____
_____
_____

WHEN I FEEL LEFT OUT
WEEK 23

BIBLE VERSE:

"Be strong and brave. Don't be afraid of them. Don't be frightened. The Lord your God will go with you. He will not leave you or forget you." – Deuteronomy 31:6.

DEVOTIONAL THOUGHT:
Sometimes you might feel like everyone else has someone to play with or talk to, and you're left alone. It can make your heart feel sad. But you are never truly alone, because Jesus is always with you even when others forget or ignore you.

Feeling left out can also happen when you choose to do what is right, but others decide to do the wrong thing. Choosing to live God's way means there will be times you have to stand alone or be part of a smaller group. That can feel hard, but Jesus is happy when you choose His way.

When you feel left out, remember that Jesus understands how that feels. There were times people didn't listen to Him or walked away, but He never stopped loving them. Jesus has promised to always stay close to you. You are special to Him, and He has a wonderful plan that includes you.

What to Do When You Feel Left Out:
Ask God to make you strong.

Ask God to make you brave.

Ask God to fill your heart with His love.

Pray that God will send you kind friends who love Him too.

You can also look around and see if someone else is alone; go to them, share a smile, and be their friend. Sometimes the best way to stop feeling left out is to help someone else feel loved.

LESSON / REFLECTION:
Even when I feel left out, Jesus is always with me, and He will send me the right friends.

PRAYER:
Dear Jesus, thank You for always being with me. When I feel lonely or left out, make me strong and brave. Fill my heart with Your love and give me good friends who love You too. In Jesus name I ask, Amen.

ACTIVITY / THOUGHT FOR THE WEEK:
If you see someone sitting alone at school or church, go and say hello or share something with them.
Write or draw one way you can help someone feel included this week.

VERSE TO REMEMBER:

"The Lord Himself will go before you. He will be with you; He will never leave you or forget you." – Deuteronomy 31:8.

_____

_____

_____

USING MY GIFTS FOR GOD
WEEK 24

BIBLE VERSE:

"Much is required from the person to whom much is given; much more is required from the person to whom much more is given. – Luke 12:48b GNT

DEVOTIONAL THOUGHT:
God has given everyone something special. Some people can sing, some can draw, some can write, some can dance, some can carve, some can mould, some can build, some can make others laugh, and some can help others learn easily. Some love to help or take care of others. These are called talents or gifts.

"Ms Debola, why did God give us gifts?"

God gave you gifts so that you can use them to help others, and to make Him happy. When you use your gifts to do good, you are serving God. It doesn't matter if your talent feels small, it is special to God when you use it well.

Even children in the Bible used their gifts. David used his skill with a sling and his courage to face Goliath. A young boy gave his lunch to Jesus, and it fed thousands of people! Your gift, no matter how small it seems, can make a big difference when you give it to God.

Open your bible to, and read Exodus 31:1-11, these verses are talking about how God chose two men named Bezalel

and Oholiab. God filled them with His Spirit and gave them special skills.

They knew how to make beautiful things, build, design, carve, and create amazing crafts for God's house. God Himself taught them and gave them wisdom to do excellent work.

This shows us that God doesn't give gifts only to pastors, singers, or prophets. He also gives gifts to people who draw, paint, build, sew, design, craft, or create things. God still gives these abilities today. If you love drawing, building with blocks, making things with your hands, or creating designs, God is willing and ready to help you become even better. He can use your gifts to make the world a better place and for His glory. Remember, the gifts and talents God gives you are not just for fun. One day, you will tell God how you used them. God wants you to use your gifts well, not hide them or ignore them. He wants you to grow, practice, and use your skills to help others and make Him happy.

The Bible says in Matthew 25:21 ICB: *"The master answered, 'You did well. You are a good servant who can be trusted. You did well with small things. So, I will let you care for much greater things. Come share my happiness with me'"*. This means when you use the gifts God gave you, He is pleased, and He trusts you with even more.

If you're not sure what your gift is yet, ask God to show you. Try new things, learn new skills, and ask your parents or teachers what they see you doing well.

LESSON / REFLECTION:
My talents are gifts from God. I will use them to help others and make God proud.

PRAYER:
Dear God, thank You for the gifts and talents You have given me. Please help me to discover them and use them to bless others.

Teach me to always do everything for Your glory. In Jesus name I ask, Amen.

ACTIVITY / THOUGHT FOR THE WEEK:
With the help of your parent or guardian, write or draw one or more of your talents. Think of one way you can use each of them this week at home, in school, in your activity club, or in church.

In the verse below, replace "Bezalel" with your own name, replace "I" with God; and say the words to yourself again and again.

VERSE TO REMEMBER:

"I have filled Bezalel with the Spirit of God. I have given him the skill, ability and knowledge to do all kinds of work. Exodus 31: 3.

USING MY MONEY GOD'S WAY

WEEK 25

BIBLE VERSE:

"'The silver is mine, and the gold is mine,' says the Lord of heaven's armies." – Haggai 2:8

DEVOTIONAL THOUGHT:
Money comes from God. Yes, your parents, aunties, or uncles may give you some, but they are only the channels God uses to bless you. God is the owner and real giver of everything including money.

"Ms Debola, does God care how I use my money?"

Yes, He does! God wants us to use money wisely. When we learn to manage it well, we show Him that we can be trusted with more.

There's a wise money idea called the **Five Jars** that helps us remember how to use money in a godly way. Imagine you have five jars, and whenever you get money like a gift or pocket money you can divide it into these jars:

1. God's Jar – Giving: This is the first and most important jar. You give to God through your tithes and offering. Tithe is simply the first 10% of any amount that comes into your hand/bank account, while offering is a gift presented to God as an act of worship and thanksgiving. Giving to God simply means you put Him first (Tithes) and you are thankful that you belong to Him (Offering).

2. Saving Jar: This is for keeping some money aside for later. It teaches patience and planning.
3. Spending Jar: This is for things you can buy now, like snacks or small treats.
4. Helping Jar: This is for blessing others maybe giving a friend lunch, supporting a cause, or helping at church.
5. Learning Jar: This is for books, tools, or things that help you grow your mind and gifts.

When you use money this way, you are honouring God with wisdom. Remember, the Bible says: "Whoever can be trusted with small things can also be trusted with large things. Whoever is dishonest in little things will be dishonest in large things too." – Luke 16:10

LESSON / REFLECTION:
God gave me money to use wisely. I will honour Him first, save, share, and spend carefully.

PRAYER:
Dear God, thank You for providing for me and my family. Please teach me to use my money wisely. Help me to give to You first, to save, and to help others. Let everything I have bring You glory. In Jesus name I ask, Amen.

ACTIVITY / THOUGHT FOR THE WEEK:
With the help of your parent or guardian, make your own Five Jars using small containers or envelopes. Label them God's Jar, Saving, Spending, Helping, and Learning. Each time you receive money, divide it into the jars. Watch how God blesses your faithfulness.

VERSE TO REMEMBER:

You might say to yourself, "I am rich because of my own strength and power." But remember the Lord your God! It is He who gives the power to become rich. He keeps the agreement He promised to your ancestors. So it is today. – Deuteronomy 8:17-18.

PRAISING AND WORSHIPPING GOD   WEEK 26

BIBLE VERSE:

"Come, let's bow down and worship Him. Let us kneel before the Lord who made us." – Psalm 95:6

DEVOTIONAL THOUGHT:
Praising and worshipping God means showing Him how much you love Him. You praise God by singing, clapping, dancing, and smiling while thinking about His goodness. You worship God by thanking Him for who He is – kind, powerful, loving, and holy.

"Ms Debola, is worship only singing?"

No, worship is more than singing, but you should still sing to Him. It is how you live every day obeying God, loving others, and doing what pleases Him. When you pray, help others, or say "thank You Jesus," you are also worshipping God.

David loved to sing and dance before God. He didn't care who was watching because his heart was full of love for the Lord. You can worship like David with joy, honesty, and love.

LESSON / REFLECTION:
I will worship God with my songs, my heart, and my actions.

PRAYER:

Dear God, thank You for being so good to me. Please teach me to worship You in everything I do. Help me to love You with all my heart, with all my soul, and with all my strength. In Jesus name I ask, Amen.

ACTIVITY / THOUGHT FOR THE WEEK:

Pick one song to sing to God every morning or evening this week. You can clap, dance, or play an instrument if you like. Tell God why you love Him.

VERSE TO REMEMBER:

"Let everything that has breath praise the Lord. Praise the Lord!" – Psalm 150:6.

LEARNING TO BE PATIENT
WEEK 27

BIBLE VERSE:

"Be joyful because you have hope. Be patient when trouble comes. Pray at all times." – Romans 12:12.

DEVOTIONAL THOUGHT:
Patience means waiting with a good attitude. It means staying calm and trusting that things will happen at the right time. Sometimes, you might pray for something and not get it immediately. That does not mean God forgot it means He knows the best time to answer.

"Ms Debola, what if I really want it now?"

It's okay to want something, but God wants us to learn to wait and trust Him. When you rush or get angry, you miss the lesson He's teaching you. Patience helps you grow stronger and wiser.

Patience is also about how you treat people. Sometimes your friend, parent, or sibling might take time to do what you asked, or they might have a habit that annoys you. Being patient means not shouting, complaining, or giving up on them. Instead, you can talk kindly, pray for them, and give them time to grow or learn.

God is patient with us every day. He forgives us and helps us become better. When we show patience to others, we are acting like God and spreading His love.

Think about a seed when it's planted, it doesn't grow into a tree right away. It takes time, sunlight, and care. In the same way, some blessings take time to grow, and people also take time to change. Waiting helps your faith grow deeper and your heart grow gentler.

LESSON / REFLECTION:
I will be patient with God's timing and with the people around me.

PRAYER:
Dear God, thank You for being patient with me. Please help me to be patient with others too. Teach me to wait for Your timing, to stay calm when I have to wait, and to speak kindly when people take time to change. In Jesus name I ask, Amen.

ACTIVITY / THOUGHT FOR THE WEEK:
Think of one thing you've been waiting for. Each day this week, thank God for it and tell Him you trust His timing. Also, think of one person who sometimes makes it hard for you to stay calm. Pray for him/her and look for one kind thing to say to or do for him/her this week.

VERSE TO REMEMBER:

"But the Spirit gives love, joy, peace, patience, kindness, goodness, faithfulness, gentleness, self-control. There is no law that says these things are wrong." – Galatians 5:22–23.

_____
_____
_____
_____
_____
_____

CONTROLLING MY ANGER

WEEK 28

BIBLE VERSE:

"When you are angry, do not sin. And do not go on being angry all day." – Ephesians 4:26.

DEVOTIONAL THOUGHT:

Everyone gets angry sometimes. Even Jesus felt angry when people disrespected God's temple. But the difference is that Jesus didn't let His anger make Him do something wrong. God gave us emotions, but He also wants us to learn how to control them.

Anger is only a feeling. It does not own you, and it does not define who you are. You are not an angry person you are a child of God who can choose peace and kindness instead of anger.

"Ma, what if someone makes me really angry?"

When you feel angry, **the first thing to do is stop and breathe**. Don't shout or hit anyone. You can walk away for a moment and talk to God quietly in your heart. Say, **"Lord, please help me calm down."**

Anger becomes a problem when it makes you say or do hurtful things. The Bible says; we should not let the sun go down while we are still angry, that means we should forgive quickly and not stay upset for too long.

If someone offends you, tell him/her calmly how you feel or talk to a trusted adult. Holding on to anger only makes your heart heavy. But when you forgive, your heart feels light and peaceful again.

LESSON / REFLECTION:
Anger is just a feeling. It does not control me. It does not own me. I will choose peace, forgive quickly, and act with love. I am not an angry person.

PRAYER:
Dear Jesus, thank You for teaching me how to control my anger. Please help me to stay calm when I'm upset. Remind me that anger does not define me and that I can choose peace and love. In Jesus name I ask, Amen.

ACTIVITY / THOUGHT FOR THE WEEK:
Think about something that recently made you angry. Ask God to help you forgive and forget it. Each time you feel angry this week, stop, take a deep breath and whisper "God, please help me stay calm" and then count from one to ten, taking deep breaths.

VERSE TO REMEMBER:

"A person who quickly gets angry causes trouble. But a person who controls his temper stops a quarrel." – Proverbs 15:18.

_____
_____
_____
_____
_____
_____
_____

CHOOSING JOY EVERYDAY

WEEK 29

BIBLE VERSE:

"Be full of joy in the Lord always. I will say it again. Be full of joy." – Philippians 4:4.

DEVOTIONAL THOUGHT:

Joy is not the same as happiness. Happiness comes and goes depending on what is happening around us; like when you get a gift, play your favourite game, or eat your favourite food. But joy comes from God, and it stays in your heart even when things are not perfect.

"Ma, how can I have joy when things go wrong?"

You can choose joy by remembering that God is always with you. Joy says, "I may not like what is happening, but I still trust God." Even when things don't go your way, you can smile, sing, or say a thankful prayer because you know that God's plan is still good.

Joy is also something you share with others. When you smile, encourage, or help someone, you are spreading God's joy. The Bible says that joy is one of the fruits of the Spirit, that means it grows in your heart when you walk with God.

LESSON / REFLECTION:

Joy is a gift from God that stays no matter what happens. I will choose joy every day.

PRAYER:
Dear God, thank You for giving me joy. Please help me to remember that real joy comes from You and not from things. Teach me to choose joy even when things don't go my way, and to share that joy with others. In Jesus name I ask, Amen.

ACTIVITY / THOUGHT FOR THE WEEK:
Think of three things that make you smile and thank God for them. Each morning, say, "Today, I choose joy!" and look for one way to make someone else smile.

VERSE TO REMEMBER:

"You will teach me God's way to live. Being with You will fill me with joy. At your right hand I will find pleasure forever." – Psalms 16:11.

_____
_____
_____
_____
_____
_____
_____
_____
_____
_____
_____
_____
_____
_____

LEARNING TO SAY SORRY

WEEK 30

BIBLE VERSE:

"But if we confess our sins, he will forgive our sins. We can trust God. He does what is right. He will make us clean from all the wrongs we have done." – 1 John 1:9.

DEVOTIONAL THOUGHT:
Everyone makes mistakes sometimes. Maybe you shouted at someone, disobeyed your parents, took what didn't belong to you, lied, or were rude to a friend. All these things are sins, and they displease Jesus. But the good news is that, Jesus is always ready to forgive when we say sorry and truly mean it.

"Ms Debola, what if I keep making the same mistake?"

Jesus knows you are still learning. He wants you to keep trying and to talk to Him whenever you fall. Saying sorry means, you understand that what you did was wrong and that you want to do better next time. Saying sorry does not make you weak; it shows you have a humble and brave heart. When you say sorry to Jesus, you are admitting that you need His help. When you say sorry to people, you are choosing peace instead of pride.

Remember, Jesus is pleased with children who keep their promises, tell the truth, and admit when they are wrong.

PRAYER:
Dear Jesus, thank You for always forgiving me when I say sorry. Please help me to obey You, honour my parents, and tell the truth. Teach me to say sorry quickly when I do wrong and to live in a way that pleases You. In Jesus name I ask, Amen.

ACTIVITY / THOUGHT FOR THE WEEK:
Think about something you've done that may have hurt someone or disobeyed God. Talk to Jesus about it and ask Him to forgive you. If you need to, go to the person and say, "I'm sorry." Then think of one way to do better next time.

> **VERSE TO REMEMBER:**
>
> *I confess my iniquity; I am sorry for my sin.*
> *Psalms 38:18 ESV.*

BEING HUMBLE: NOT PROUD

WEEK 31

BIBLE VERSE:

"But God gives us even more grace, as the scripture says; God is against the proud, but he gives grace to the humble." – James 4:6.

DEVOTIONAL THOUGHT:

Being humble doesn't mean letting people treat you badly or thinking you are not good enough. It also means being kind and gentle, even when you know you are really good at something or you have special things that others don't. You should say "Thank You, Lord," Instead of "Look at me!"

"Ms Debola, does that mean I shouldn't feel good about what I do?"

No, it's good to be happy about what you do well. But humility means giving God the glory for it. You can say, "God helped me do this!" instead of taking all the praise for yourself. Pride makes people think they don't need help or correction. But humility helps you learn, grow, and work well with others. Even Jesus, the Son of God, was; Humble He served others, helped the poor, and obeyed His Father. When you are humble, you listen, you share, you apologise, and you treat others kindly. God is very happy when His children walk in humility.

LESSON / REFLECTION:

Everything I have comes from God. I will be humble, kind, and thankful.

PRAYER:
Dear God, thank You for every gift and special help You've given me. Please help me not to be proud or boastful. Teach me to stay humble, to honour others, and to always give You the glory. In Jesus name I ask, Amen.

ACTIVITY / THOUGHT FOR THE WEEK:
Think of something you are good at; maybe singing, reading, or drawing. This week, thank God for helping you do it. Then find a way to use that gift to help or encourage someone else.

VERSE TO REMEMBER:

"When you do things, do not let selfishness or pride be your guide. Be humble and give more honour to others than to yourselves." – Philippians 2:3.

USING KIND WORDS
BIBLE VERSE:

WEEK 32

"Pleasant words are like a honeycomb. They make a person happy and healthy." – Proverbs 16:24.

DEVOTIONAL THOUGHT:

Words are powerful. The things you say can make someone happy, or they can make someone sad. God wants you to use your words to help, encourage, and bring peace to others.

"Ms Debola, what if someone is mean to me first?"

Even when others say unkind things, you can still choose to speak kindly. You should not accept or believe the mean things people say about you. You can kindly say, "That's not true," and walk away without being rude. And if you walk away, tell yourself in your heart, "I don't believe those words," and think about what God says about you instead.

Kind words show that your heart belongs to God. When you speak kindly to your parents, friends, teachers, and even your siblings, you make God smile. You also make your world brighter!

Before you speak, think: **Are my words true? Are they kind? Will they help or hurt?** If the words don't build others up, it's better not to say them.

LESSON / REFLECTION:
My words are a gift. I will use them to spread kindness and peace.

PRAYER:
Dear God, thank You for giving me a voice. Please help me to use my words to bless others. Teach me to speak kindly, to stay calm, and to bring joy to those around me. In Jesus name I ask, Amen.

ACTIVITY / THOUGHT FOR THE WEEK:
Each day this week, find one person you can encourage with kind words; it could be your parent, teacher, or friend. Watch how your kind words make them smile!

> **VERSE TO REMEMBER:**
>
> *"When you talk, do not say harmful things. But say what people need – words that will help others become stronger. Then what you say will help those who listen to you." – Ephesians 4:29.*

_____
_____
_____
_____
_____
_____
_____
_____
_____
_____
_____

SPEAKING GOD'S WORD OVER MYSELF — WEEK 33

BIBLE VERSE:

"What you say can mean life or death. Those who love to talk will be rewarded for what they say." – Proverbs 18:21

DEVOTIONAL THOUGHT:

Your words are powerful. When you speak, your words can build up or break down. That's why God wants you to use your mouth to say good things especially His word, over yourself.

"Ms Debola, why do I have to say it over myself?"

Because when you speak God's word, your own ears hear it. It helps your heart believe it, and it reminds you of what God has said about you. When you say what God says, you are agreeing with Him!

If you wake up and say, "I am blessed," "God loves me," "I can do all things through Christ," or "I am strong in the Lord," you are speaking life upon yourself. Those are not just words, they are God's truth.

Even Jesus spoke God's word when the devil tried to tempt Him. Each time, He said, "It is written." That's how powerful God's word is when it comes out of your mouth.

LESSON / REFLECTION:
I will speak God's word over myself every day. I will say what God says about me.

PRAYER:
Dear God, thank You for giving me Your word. Help me to use my mouth to speak what You say, not what I feel. Teach me to confess Your truth every day so my heart will stay full of faith and joy. In Jesus name I ask, Amen.

ACTIVITY / THOUGHT FOR THE WEEK:
Each morning, say these words out loud:

God loves me.
I am special and wanted. I have a special sparkle.
My body is strong and healthy.

You can also write your favourite verses and keep them where you can see them and confess them daily.

> **VERSE TO REMEMBER:**
> *"It is written in the Scriptures, "I believed, so I spoke." Our faith is like this, too. We believe, and so we speak. I believed, so I spoke." – 2 Corinthians 4:13.*

_____
_____
_____
_____
_____
_____

SERVING GOD WITH A HAPPY HEART
WEEK 34

BIBLE VERSE:

"Serve the Lord with joy; come before him with singing." – Psalm 100:2.

DEVOTIONAL THOUGHT:

Serving the Lord Jesus means doing what pleases Him and using your gifts to honour Him. You can serve Jesus with your gifts, your body, your time, what you know, and what you have.

"Ms Debola, how do I serve Jesus if I'm still little?"

You can serve Jesus right where you are now! You can serve Him by worshipping with all your heart, reading your Bible, praying, and helping where you can. When you serve joyfully, you show Jesus that you love Him.

Serving in your own little way also means helping with your little hands in church with the help of grown-ups. You can pick up litter, hold small items, greet people with a big smile, draw pictures to appreciate others, or ask grown-ups serving in church how you can help.

Sometimes serving may feel tiring or unnoticed, but Jesus always sees. He rewards those who serve Him sincerely. Serving Jesus should never feel like a chore, it's a way to say, "Thank You, Lord, for loving me."

LESSON / REFLECTION:
Serving the Lord Jesus is my way of showing love to Him. I will serve with joy, not with complaints.

PRAYER:
Dear Jesus, thank You for choosing me to serve You. Please help me to serve You with my hands, my time, and my gifts. Teach me to do everything with joy and love, so You will be pleased with me. In Jesus name I ask, Amen.

ACTIVITY / THOUGHT FOR THE WEEK:
This week, find one way to serve in church or at home: pick up litter, smile at someone, or help a grown-up. Say, "Lord, I'm happy to serve You!"

VERSE TO REMEMBER:

"Do not be lazy but work hard. Serve the Lord with all your heart." – Romans 12:11.

_____
_____
_____
_____
_____
_____
_____
_____
_____
_____

DISOBEDIENCE AND ITS CONSEQUENCES   WEEK 35
BIBLE VERSE:

"Do not let anyone fool you by telling you things that are not true. These things will bring God's anger on those who do not obey Him." – Ephesians 5:6.

DEVOTIONAL THOUGHT:
Disobedience means knowing what to do and choosing not to do it. When we disobey God or our parents, it displeases God and can bring unpleasantness.

Think about Jonah; God told him to go to Nineveh, but he ran the other way. What happened? He ended up in the belly of a big fish! (Jonah 1–2). God didn't leave Jonah there because He hated him. He wanted Jonah to learn that obeying is always better.

When we obey, things go smoothly. But when we disobey, it often causes problems at home, in school, and even in our hearts. God corrects us because He loves us and wants us to grow into wise and happy people.

LESSON / REFLECTION:
Obedience brings blessings. Disobedience brings rebuke.

PRAYER:
Dear God, thank You for loving me enough to correct me when I'm wrong.

Please help me to obey You, my parents, and everyone You've placed over me. Give me a heart that listens and a spirit that does what is right. In Jesus name I ask, Amen.

ACTIVITY / THOUGHT FOR THE WEEK:

Think about one time you disobeyed and what happened after. Write or draw how you could have obeyed instead. Ask God to help you make better choices next time.

> **VERSE TO REMEMBER:**
> *"Children, obey your parents the way the Lord wants, because this is the right thing to do." – Ephesians 6:1.*

_____

_____

_____

_____

_____

_____

_____

_____

_____

_____

_____

_____

_____

_____

_____

FAITH MAKES ME STRONG

WEEK 36

BIBLE VERSE:

"Faith is what makes real the things we hope for. It is proof of what we cannot see." – Hebrews 11:1.

DEVOTIONAL THOUGHT:

Faith is trusting God even when you can't see how things will happen. It is like planting a seed; you can't see what's happening under the ground, but you believe a plant will grow.

Ms Debola, the Bible says faith means being sure. What happens when I'm not sure? What if I doubt?

We are not always sure; sometimes we doubt. But just like when you plant a seed and you want to check if it's growing, you might feel like digging it up to see; but that's bad for the seed! It needs time and trust. Faith works the same way. When we pray or when God tells us something, even if we don't understand everything, we don't say, "I'm not sure. Will it ever happen?" We say what God has said to us or what we prayed for aloud. We say it to ourselves again and again, and we give God thanks because His word is true.

Faith helps you stay strong when things are tough, when the answer seems slow, or when you don't understand why something happened. People like Abraham, Moses, and Daniel all had faith. They trusted God, and He made them strong and helped them win.

LESSON / REFLECTION:
Faith makes me strong because I know God always keeps His promises.

PRAYER:
Dear God, thank You for giving me faith. Help me to trust You even when I can't see the answer yet. Make my faith strong every day. In Jesus name I ask, Amen.

ACTIVITY / THOUGHT FOR THE WEEK:
Draw something you are believing God for like healing, good grades, peace at home, or a new friend. Each time you see your drawing, say what you want aloud to yourself and say, "I believe God will do it."

VERSE TO REMEMBER:

"Without faith no one can please God. Whoever comes to God must believe that He is real and that He rewards those who truly want to find Him." – Hebrews 11:6.

_____
_____
_____
_____
_____
_____
_____
_____
_____
_____

THE HOLYSPIRIT HELPS ME

WEEK 37

BIBLE VERSE:

"But the Helper will teach you everything. He will cause you to remember all the things I told you. This Helper is the Holy Spirit whom the Father will send in My name." – John 14:26.

DEVOTIONAL THOUGHT:

When Jesus went back to heaven, He didn't leave us alone. He sent the Holy Spirit to help us every day. The Holy Spirit is our Helper, Teacher, and Friend. He helps us understand the Bible, reminds us to do what is right, and gives us peace when we're sad or afraid. The Holy Spirit lives inside everyone who believes in Jesus, yes, even children like you!

Ms Debola, the Holy Spirit lives inside me? Will He come out one day like a baby?

No, the Holy Spirit stays inside you forever. But He shows Himself to you and through you every day. He talks to you by putting good thoughts in your heart, reminding you of what the Bible says, or making you feel peaceful when you obey God.

How will I know when the Holy Spirit is talking to me?

You'll know because what He says will always agree with the word of God and help you do what is right. The Holy Spirit never says anything bad or confusing. He always helps you love God more and love others better.

LESSON / REFLECTION:
The Holy Spirit is my Helper. I will listen to His voice and follow His leading.

PRAYER:
Dear Holy Spirit, thank You for living in me. Please help me remember God's word, obey quickly, and stay full of Your peace and joy. Teach me to listen to You always. In Jesus name I ask, Amen.

ACTIVITY / THOUGHT FOR THE WEEK:
Each morning, ask the Holy Spirit to help you with something; maybe to be kind, to pray and study the word better, pay attention in class, or share with someone, At the end of the week, thank Him for helping you.

VERSE TO REMEMBER:

"Also, the Spirit helps us. We are very weak, but the Spirit helps us with our weakness. We do not know how to pray as we should. But the Spirit Himself speaks to God for us, even begs God for us. The Spirit speaks to God with deep feelings that word cannot explain." – Romans 8:26.

_____

_____

_____

_____

_____

_____

_____

_____

GOD HEARS ME WHEN I PRAY

WEEK 38

BIBLE VERSE:

"We can come to God with no doubts. This means that when we ask God for things, and those things agree with what God wants for us, then God cares about what we say. God listens to us every time we ask Him. So, we know that He gives us the things that we ask from Him." – 1 John 5:14-15.

DEVOTIONAL THOUGHT:

When you talk to God, He listens. God never sleeps or gets too busy to hears you. Even if you whisper a small prayer, He hears every word and knows exactly how you feel (Hebrews 4:15).

Sometimes it may seem like God is quiet, but He always hears and answers in the best way: maybe yes, a no, a wait a little while. He always gives what is best for you, even when it's not what you expected.

"Ms Debola, what if I don't see anything happen?"

You should keep praying and believing. Just because you can't see it doesn't mean God isn't working. Remember Daniel? God heard him from the very first day he prayed, even before the answer came. The Bible says, "Since the first day that you set your mind to understand and to humble yourself before your God, your words were heard." (Daniel 10:12) God always hear His children.

LESSON / REFLECTION:

God hears me every time I pray. I will keep talking to Him and trust His answer.

PRAYER:

Dear God, thank You for always hearing me when I pray. Help me to trust Your timing and to believe that You know what is best for me. Thank You for loving me and for never ignoring my voice. In Jesus name I ask, Amen.

ACTIVITY / THOUGHT FOR THE WEEK:

With the help of your parent or guardian, write or draw three prayers you have prayed before and how God answered them or how you are still waiting. Thank Him for hearing you and working things out for your good.

VERSE TO REMEMBER:

I will provide for their needs before they ask. I will help them while they are still asking for help. Isaiah 65:24.

_____

_____

_____

_____

_____

_____

_____

_____

_____

_____

_____

_____

RESPECTING TEACHERS AND LEADERS WEEK 39
BIBLE VERSE:

"Show respect for all people. Love the brothers and sisters of God's family. Respect God. Honour the king." – 1 Peter 2:17.

DEVOTIONAL THOUGHT:
God places people in our lives to guide and teach us; our parents, teachers, pastors, and other leaders. They help us learn what is right and make good choices. When you respect them, you are also showing respect to God because He is the One who put them in charge to help you grow.

Ms Debola, what does it mean to respect my teacher or leader?

It means you listen when they speak, follow instructions even when it's not easy, and speak politely. Sometimes you might not agree with what they say, but you should still respond kindly.

What if my teacher or an adult asks me to do what I know is wrong?

That can happen too. You should politely explain and insist that you cannot do what you have been asked to do, as you believe it is wrong. Then tell your parents or pastor so they can guide you. God is pleased when you obey Him first and stay respectful at the same time. Respect shows that your heart is humble, kind, and ready to learn.

LESSON / REFLECTION:
I will respect the people God has placed over me and honour them with my words and actions.

PRAYER:
Dear God, thank You for the people who teach me and guide me. Help me to listen, learn, and show respect in everything I do. Give me wisdom to make the right choices when I'm unsure. In Jesus name I ask, Amen.

ACTIVITY / THOUGHT FOR THE WEEK:
Think of one teacher, pastor, or leader you're grateful for. Make them a small note or drawing to say, "Thank you for teaching me."

VERSE TO REMEMBER:

"Obey your leaders and be under their authority. These men are watching you because they are responsible for your souls. Obey them so that they will do this work with joy, not sadness. It will not help you to make their work hard." – Hebrews 13:17.

_____

_____

_____

_____

_____

_____

_____

_____

_____

_____

CHOOSE GOD, NOT MAGIC
(WITCHCRAFT AND DARK POWERS)

WEEK 40

BIBLE VERSE:

"Don't let anyone use magic or witchcraft. No one should try to explain the meaning of signs. Don't let anyone try to control others with magic. Don't let them be mediums or try to talk with the spirits of dead people. The Lord hates anyone who does these things." – Deuteronomy 18:10b–12a.

DEVOTIONAL THOUGHT:

Some people try to use magic, witchcraft, spells, or special powers to make things happen. You might even see these things in movies, cartoons, games, schools, or stores. But those powers don't come from God. They come from dark and evil places that God tells us to stay away from.

God's children don't need magic or witchcraft because God's power is greater than any other power. When you pray, speak God's word, or sing in Jesus' name, you are using the strongest power God's power.

Ms Debola, what if it looks fun or good in a movie?

That's how the devil tricks people he makes what is wrong look exciting or harmless. But anything that invites darkness, spirits, or magic is not from God. We should never play, watch, or join anything that teaches us to do or say what God says not to.

Ms Debola, what if I don't want to use the powers, but I just like the fun, the movements, or the dressing, and I want to try?

It is still participation, which means joining in and encouraging evil. Even dressing up or role-playing as witches, ghosts, or other dark things is not harmless fun, it is pretending to be a part of what God hates. **When you pretend to do what is wrong, your heart slowly becomes less careful about what pleases God.**

Instead of copying those things, enjoy the light, joy, and beauty that come from God. You can dress as God's child full of joy, faith, and love and share His light wherever you go. **Choosing God means trusting His word, His Spirit, and His power only.** When you follow Jesus, you are already full of light and light is always stronger than darkness!

LESSON / REFLECTION:
I will stay away from anything that uses magic, witchcraft, or dark powers. I will always choose God's light and truth.

PRAYER:
Dear Jesus, thank You for Your great power that lives in me. Help me to always choose You and stay far from magic, witchcraft, or anything that is not from You. Fill me with Your light and joy so I can shine bright for You every day. In Jesus name I ask, Amen.

ACTIVITY / THOUGHT FOR THE WEEK:
With the help of your parent or guardian, look through your books, games, TV channels and shows. **If you find anything that celebrates witchcraft, magic, or dark things, choose to remove it.** Ask God to fill your heart and home with songs, words, and pictures that shine with His light.

VERSE TO REMEMBER:

"Lord, there is no god like You. There are no works like Yours." – Psalm 86:8.

CHOOSING LIGHT, NOT DARKNESS

WEEK 41

BIBLE VERSE:

"In the past you were full of darkness, but now you are full of light in the Lord. So, live like children who belong to the light." – Ephesians 5:8.

DEVOTIONAL THOUGHT:
God is light, and everyone who belongs to Him carries His light inside their heart. But there are things in the world that try to hide that light: things that celebrate fear, darkness, ghosts, and evil. Sometimes people even have parties or wear costumes to look like those things, especially around Halloween season.

Ms Debola, what's wrong with that? It's just fun!

Not everything that looks fun is good. Some things that look like fun are really ways the devil tries to make darkness seem exciting. But God wants His children to choose light to fill their hearts with love, peace, and joy, not fear or darkness.

Ms Debola, since these things are evil, can I think the people doing them are evil too? Should I tell them they are evil?

No, as the light of God, you should not do that. Not everyone doing what is wrong is a bad person, many do not just know the truth. Do not call them evil nor tell others they are evil, as they might not even know that what they are doing is wrong.

The best thing you can do is to pray for them in secret, ask God to help them see His light.

Light and darkness do not mix. When you choose to live in God's light, you're choosing truth, kindness, forgiveness, and joy. When others are dressing like scary things, you can show God's light by being kind, smiling, praying for them, singing, reading your Bible and thanking God for saving you.

You don't have to join in to fit in, you already belong to Jesus!

LESSON / REFLECTION:
I belong to God, so I will live in His light and stay away from anything that celebrates darkness or fear.

PRAYER:
Dear Jesus, thank You for filling me with Your light, help me to shine brightly wherever I go. Help me to be kind to others, and to pray for them instead of judging them. Let Your light in me help others see how good You are. In Jesus name I ask, Amen.

ACTIVITY / THOUGHT FOR THE WEEK:
With the help of a grown-up, think of three ways you can shine God's light this week.

> *"The Light shines in the darkness, and the darkness has not overpowered the Light." – John 1:5.*

_____
_____
_____

GUARDING WHAT I WATCH AND HEAR — WEEK 42

BIBLE VERSE:

"I will not look at anything wicked. I hate those who turn against God. I will have nothing to do with them." – Psalm 101:3.

DEVOTIONAL THOUGHT:
That's why it's so important to be careful about what you watch, read, and listen to. Some things on TV, the internet, or even in songs may look or sound fun, but they might not please God. They can fill your mind with fear, anger, bad words, or wrong ideas.

But when you choose godly things; songs about Bible stories, or shows that teach kindness, truth and academics, your heart becomes stronger and brighter.

Ms Debola, how can I know what is good or bad for me to watch and listen to?

Ask yourself:
Does this make me kind and respectful to my family and others?
Does this help me learn good things that make me wiser?
Does this make me feel peaceful, or does it make me angry or scared?
Would I watch this if Jesus were sitting beside me?
Does this make me love Jesus and others more?
Your honest answers to these questions will guide what you watch and hear from now on.

God wants His children to fill their hearts with good things, because what we watch and hear can shape who we become.

LESSON / REFLECTION:
I will choose to watch and listen to things that make my heart pure and my mind full of God's truth.

PRAYER:
Dear Jesus, help me to guard my eyes and ears. Teach me to say no to anything that does not please You. Fill my heart with good thoughts and pure words. Let everything I see and hear draw me closer to You. In Jesus name I ask, Amen.

ACTIVITY / THOUGHT FOR THE WEEK:
Look through the things you watch, read or listen to; your songs, cartoons, or shows. With the help of a grown-up, remove anything that doesn't please God. Find one new godly song, story, or video to enjoy this week.

> **VERSE TO REMEMBER:**
>
> *"Brothers, continue to think about the things that are good and worthy of praise. Think about the things that are true and honourable and pure and beautiful and respected." – Philippians 4:8.*

_____
_____
_____
_____
_____
_____
_____

WHEN I AM AFRAID

WEEK 43

BIBLE VERSE:

"I leave you peace. My peace I give you. I do not give it to you as the world does. So don't let your hearts be troubled. Don't be afraid." – John 14:27.

DEVOTIONAL THOUGHT:
Everyone feels afraid sometimes. Maybe you hear a strange noise at night, have a bad dream, or worry about something new at school. Even grown-ups feel afraid sometimes, but we don't let fear stop us, because God is always with us.

Before Jesus went back to heaven, He gave His friends a (special gift:) His peace. Peace means a calm heart that knows everything will be okay because God is in control. Jesus said, "My peace I give you." That means we don't have to live in fear; we can rest knowing that Jesus is watching over us.

Ms Debola, what should I do when I get scared?

You should talk to God right away. You can say, "God, I'm scared right now. Please give me Your peace."

God's peace is like a soft, warm blanket that covers your heart and makes you calm inside. You can also speak God's word when you're afraid. Say, "Jesus is with me. I will not be afraid." When you remember what God says, fear begins to disappear.

Maybe your sick friend whom you hoped would get well didn't get well, or something didn't go the way you prayed, that can make your heart afraid or sad. But even then, Jesus is still good, and He is always near you. He gives peace to those who trust Him and never leaves their side.

LESSON / REFLECTION:
God's peace keeps my heart calm and strong, even when I feel afraid.

PRAYER:
Dear Jesus, thank You for giving me Your peace. When I feel afraid, remind me that You are with me. Help me to stay calm and trust You with all my heart. Amen.

ACTIVITY / THOUGHT FOR THE WEEK:
At bedtime, pray before you sleep and ask God to give you peaceful dreams. Write down or draw something that makes you afraid and then write beside it, **"Jesus gives me peace."**

VERSE TO REMEMBER:

"When I am afraid, I will trust in You." – Psalm 56:3

_____
_____
_____
_____
_____
_____
_____
_____

WHEN I FEEL SAD

WEEK 44

BIBLE VERSE:

"The Lord is close to the brokenhearted. He saves those whose spirits have been crushed." – Psalm 34:18.

DEVOTIONAL THOUGHT:

Everyone feels sad sometimes. Maybe your toy broke, your pet is gone, someone was unkind, or someone you love is sick. It's okay to feel sad, God understands. He doesn't get angry when you cry; instead, He comes closer to comfort you.

When your heart feels heavy, God is right there beside you. He doesn't walk away when you're sad, He stays close and helps your heart heal. That's what the Bible means when it says, "The Lord is close to the broken-hearted."

Even Jesus cried when He was sad. When His friend Lazarus died, "Jesus wept." That shows that it's okay to cry, and it doesn't mean you're weak, it means you have a healthy heart that feels love and pain.

Ms Debola, what should I do when I feel sad?

You should talk to Jesus about it. You can say, "Jesus, my heart hurts today. Please make me feel better." You can sing to Him, read a verse that reminds you of His love, or talk to your parents or teacher about how you feel. When you talk to Jesus, it's like opening the window for His sunshine to come in and chase away the sadness.

Jesus is always close to you and cares about how you feel.

LESSON / REFLECTION:
When I feel sad, I will remember that Jesus is close to me and loves me deeply.

PRAYER:
Dear Jesus, thank You for being close to me when I'm sad. Please comfort my heart and fill me with Your peace and joy again. Help me to remember that You love me and that I can always talk to You. Amen.

ACTIVITY / THOUGHT FOR THE WEEK:
Draw a picture of a rainy day and then a sunny day. Under the sunny day, write, "God's love always makes my heart bright again." Whenever you feel sad, look at it and thank Jesus for being close to you.

VERSE TO REMEMBER:

"Those who are sad now are happy. God will comfort them." Matthew 5:4.

_____
_____
_____
_____
_____
_____
_____
_____
_____

OBEYING EVEN WHEN NO ONE IS WATCHING — WEEK 45

BIBLE VERSE:

"The Lord's eyes see everything that happens. He watches both evil and good people." – Proverbs 15:3.

DEVOTIONAL THOUGHT:

It's easy to do the right thing when people are watching; when your teacher, parent, or leader is nearby. But what happens when no one is looking? Do you still obey? Do you still tell the truth?

Ms Debola, why should I still obey when no one can see me?

Because even when people don't see you, God does. His eyes are full of love, and He sees everything; not to punish you, but to guide you and help you grow. Doing what is right when no one is watching shows that your heart truly loves God.

Obeying when no one is watching also helps you build good habits.

When you learn to do your homework, clean your space, or tell the truth without being pressed for it, you're becoming a responsible and trustworthy person. Those good habits will help you do well in life and make God proud. Sometimes you might feel like no one notices the good things you do, but God sees them all, and He is happy when you choose what is right.

LESSON / REFLECTION:
I will obey and do what is right because I love God, even when no one is watching.

PRAYER:
Dear God, thank You for always watching over me with love. Help me to obey You and do the right thing, even when no one sees me. Help me to build good habits that will help me in the future. In Jesus name I ask, Amen.

ACTIVITY / THOUGHT FOR THE WEEK:
This week, do one good thing quietly, something only you and God will know. It could be helping someone, cleaning up, or saying kind words to someone who needs it.

> **VERSE TO REMEMBER:**
>
> *"No one can hide where I cannot see him," says the Lord. "I fill all of heaven and earth," says the Lord." – Jeremiah 23:24.*

_____
_____
_____
_____
_____
_____
_____
_____
_____

WORKING HARD AND DOING MY BEST — WEEK 46

BIBLE VERSE:

"Show me someone who does a good job, and I will show you someone who is better than most and worthy of the company of kings – Proverbs 22:29 GNT

DEVOTIONAL THOUGHT:
Working hard and doing your best means giving your full effort, not just doing things halfway. God wants us to do every task, homework, chores, learning a skill, or being part of an activity group with joy and excellence. When you work hard, you are not just making people proud; you are showing God that you are thankful for the gifts He has given you.

Even when no one is watching, God sees your efforts. When you do your best, you are honouring Him. Doing things with a lazy or careless attitude is never pleasing to God, but giving your best brings Him glory.

"Ma, what if I don't feel like working hard?"

You should ask God to help you. Sometimes work or study feels hard, but with God's help, you will stay focused and finish well. Remember, every good result begins with efforts. Jesus worked very hard too, He prayed, helped people, and stayed faithful to His mission. Working hard also means not giving up easily. If something is difficult, try again and trust God to give you strength.

LESSON / REFLECTION:
I will do my best in everything I do because my work is for God.

PRAYER:
Dear God, thank You for giving me strength and wisdom. Please help me to work hard and do my best in everything I do at home, in school, and in learning new skills. Let my work bring You glory and make others see Your goodness in me. In Jesus name I ask, Amen.

ACTIVITY / THOUGHT FOR THE WEEK:
Choose one thing you want to do better this week: maybe finishing your homework, cleaning your room, learning a new skill, or helping in your club or church. Write or draw how you plan to do it with joy and excellence.

VERSE TO REMEMBER:

"Being lazy will make you poor, but hard work will make you rich." – Proverbs 10:4 GNT

_____
_____
_____
_____
_____
_____
_____
_____
_____
_____
_____

AVOIDING GOSSIP

WEEK 47

BIBLE VERSE:

"An evil person causes trouble. And a person who gossips ruins friendships." – Proverbs 16:28.

DEVOTIONAL THOUGHT:

Have you ever heard someone saying unkind things about another person when that person isn't there? That's called gossip. Gossip isn't just about saying bad things it can also be sharing something that someone told you in private, or saying things you wouldn't have the courage to repeat if the person was standing in front of you.

It might seem small, but gossip can hurt people's hearts and even destroy friendships. God doesn't want us to use our mouths to spread secrets or hurtful talk. He wants our words to bring peace, truth, and love.

Ms Debola, what if someone is saying things and I just listen? I didn't say anything.

Listening to gossip is also wrong, because it keeps the bad talk going and it can corrupt your heart. You can politely say, "I don't want to talk about that," or quietly walk away, and if you cannot do any of the two, ensure it doesn't happen again by avoiding being alone with the person. Avoiding gossip doesn't make you weak it shows you are wise and kind. When you avoid gossip, you protect other people's hearts and your own.

Instead of spreading talk about others, you can use your words to share kind things, like what you love about someone or something you're thankful for.

LESSON / REFLECTION:
I will use my words to bring peace and speak kindly about others.

PRAYER:
Dear Jesus, help me not to gossip or listen to wrong talk. Teach me to use my words to show love and make peace. Let my words bring joy and encouragement to everyone around me. In Jesus name I ask, Amen.

ACTIVITY / THOUGHT FOR THE WEEK:
Think of three kind things you can say about people around you: your friends, teachers, or family. Say them this week and watch how your words spread love.

> **VERSE TO REMEMBER:**
> *"When you talk, do not say harmful things. But say what people need—words that will help others become stronger. Then what you say will help those who listen to you." – Ephesians 4:29.*

TRUSTING GOD'S PROMISES

WEEK 48

BIBLE VERSE:

"God is not a man. He will not lie. God is not a human being. He does not change His mind. What He says He will do, He does. What He promises, He keeps. – Numbers 23:19.

DEVOTIONAL THOUGHT:
People sometimes make promises they don't keep. Maybe someone said they would play with you, come to your birthday, or buy you something but they forgot. That can make you feel sad or disappointed.
But God is not like people. When God makes a promise, He always keeps it. Every word He has spoken in the Bible is true and will surely happen. If He said He will protect you, heal you, or bless you, you can believe it completely because God never breaks His word.

Ms Debola, what if it takes long for God's promise to happen?

It may not happen right away, but that doesn't mean God forgot. Sometimes God is preparing things or helping you grow before the promise comes. You should keep trusting Him by thanking Him every day and saying, "God always keep His promises to me."

When you trust God's promises, you are saying, "God, I believe You more than what I see or feel." And that kind of faith makes God smile!

LESSON / REFLECTION:
I will believe God's promises and never doubt His Word because God always tells the truth.

PRAYER:
Dear God, thank You for always keeping Your promises. Help me to trust You even when I don't see the answer right away. Teach me to believe Your Word and remember that You never lie. In Jesus name I ask, Amen.

ACTIVITY / THOUGHT FOR THE WEEK:
Find one promise of God for you in the Bible and write it on a paper or sticky note. Place it somewhere you can see every day your mirror, your bag, or your wall and say it out loud every morning.

VERSE TO REMEMBER:

"The Lord will keep His promises. With love He takes care of all He has made." – Psalms 145:13b.

_____
_____
_____
_____
_____
_____
_____
_____
_____
_____
_____
_____
_____

THANKFUL HEARTS PLEASE THE LORD. — WEEK 49

BIBLE VERSE:

"Always give thanks to God the Father for everything, in the name of our Lord Jesus Christ." – Ephesians 5:20.

DEVOTIONAL THOUGHT:
Every day, there is something to thank God for: your life, food, friends, family, school, and even the small things like laughter and sunshine. Having a thankful heart means you notice God's goodness and say, "Thank You, Lord!"

Ms Debola, what if I don't feel like saying thank You?

That happens sometimes. Maybe something didn't go your way, or you feel sad. But when you start thanking God, even when you don't feel like it, your heart becomes light and full of joy again.

Thankfulness helps you remember how good God has always been. When you complain, you forget what you already have. But when you thank God, you make Him happy because it shows you trust Him and see His blessings around you. A thankful heart pleases God!

LESSON / REFLECTION:
I will thank God for everything He has done and trust Him even when things don't go my way.

PRAYER:

Dear heavenly Father, thank You for loving me and giving me all that I need. Please forgive me when I forget to say thank You. Help me to have a heart that sees Your blessings every day and says, "Thank You Lord." In Jesus name I ask, Amen.

ACTIVITY / THOUGHT FOR THE WEEK:

Make a "Thankful Jar" with your family. Each day, write or draw one thing you are thankful for and put it inside. At the end of the week, open the jar and thank God for everything inside.

VERSE TO REMEMBER:

"Give thanks to the Lord, because He is good. His love continues forever." – Psalm 136:1.

_____
_____
_____
_____
_____
_____
_____
_____
_____
_____
_____
_____

JESUS CAME TO SAVE US

WEEK 50

BIBLE VERSE:

"The angel said to them, 'Don't be afraid. I am bringing you some good news. It will be a joy to all the people. Today your Savior was born in David's town. He is Christ, the Lord.'" – Luke 2:10–11.

DEVOTIONAL THOUGHT:
A long time ago, on a quiet night in Bethlehem, something wonderful happened. A baby named Jesus was born, but this baby was not just like any other baby. He is the Son of God who came to save the world! The angels were so happy that they sang in the sky, and one angel told the shepherds, "Do not be afraid! I bring you good news!" That good news was that Jesus came to take away our sins, to fill our hearts with peace, and to show us how much God loves us.

Ms Debola, why did Jesus have to come?

Because sin had separated people from God, and we couldn't save ourselves. But God loved us so much that He sent Jesus to bring us back to Him. When you believe in Jesus and follow Him, your heart becomes full of His light and His love. Christmas is not just about gifts, lights, or food, it is about celebrating the biggest gift ever: **Jesus! He came to save you, to live in your heart, and to make you God's child forever.**

LESSON / REFLECTION:
I am thankful that Jesus came to save me and give me new life.

PRAYER:

Dear Jesus, thank You for coming to earth for me. Thank You for saving me and showing me God's love. Help me to live in Your light every day and share Your love with others. Amen

ACTIVITY / THOUGHT FOR THE WEEK:

Draw or write about the night Jesus was born. Write "Jesus is God's gift to me" on top and thank Him every day this week for coming to save you..

> **VERSE TO REMEMBER:**
>
> *"The Son of Man came to find the lost people and save them." – Luke 19:10.*

_____
_____
_____
_____
_____
_____
_____
_____
_____
_____
_____
_____
_____
_____

GOD'S GREATEST GIFT

WEEK 51

BIBLE VERSE:

"For God loved the world so much that He gave His only Son. God gave His Son so that whoever believes in Him may not be lost, but have eternal life." – John 3:16.

DEVOTIONAL THOUGHT:

Everyone loves to receive gifts! Maybe you've gotten a toy, new clothes, or something you've always wanted. But did you know that **God gave the greatest gift ever: His Son, Jesus?** God saw that people were lost in sin and couldn't find their way back to Him. So, He sent Jesus to save us, forgive us, and show us His love. That's how much God loves you, He gave His very best!

Ms Debola, how can I receive this gift?

By believing in Jesus and asking Him to live in your heart. When you do, you become part of God's family, and His love fills your heart forever. You don't need wrapping paper or ribbons for this gift. **You just open your heart and say, "Jesus, thank You for loving me. I receive You today."**

Remember, every time you see a gift this Christmas, let it remind you of God's love, the greatest gift of all.

LESSON / REFLECTION:

I am loved by God, and I have received His greatest gift: Jesus.

PRAYER:
Dear heavenly Father, thank You for loving me so much that You gave Jesus for me. Help me to remember that Jesus is the greatest gift I could ever have. Teach me to share Your love with others this Christmas and always. In Jesus name I ask, Amen.

ACTIVITY / THOUGHT FOR THE WEEK:
Draw a big gift box and write inside it, "Jesus, God's Greatest Gift." Around it, write or draw things that show God's love family, friends, joy, peace, forgiveness, and hope.

> **VERSE TO REMEMBER:**
> *"Every good and perfect gift is from God. These good gifts come down from the Creator of the sun, moon, and stars. God does not change like their shifting shadows". – James 1:17.*

_____
_____
_____
_____
_____
_____
_____
_____
_____
_____
_____
_____
_____
_____

GOD WITH US: EMMANUEL

WEEK 52

BIBLE VERSE:

"The virgin will be pregnant. She will give birth to a son. They will name Him Immanuel." This name means 'God is with us.'"
– Matthew 1:23.

DEVOTIONAL THOUGHT:
When Jesus was born, one of His special names was Emmanuel, which means God is with us. That name reminds us that God is not far away in heaven; He came and is close to us through Jesus.

God didn't want people to feel alone, afraid, or forgotten. He wanted us to know that He is near, not just in church, but everywhere we go. So, He sent Jesus to live among us, to help us, love us, and show us who God really is.

Ms Debola, is God still with us now?

Yes, He is!

When Jesus went back to heaven, He sent the Spirit of God Himself, the Holy Spirit to stay with us forever.
So even when you can't see Him, He is right there at school, at home, when you wake up, and even when you sleep.

Ms Debola, does that mean when I see someone called Emmanuel, it's a reminder that God is with me?

That's a sweet thought! But it doesn't have to be only when you see someone named Emmanuel. God is with you all the time: when you wake up, play, study, eat, or sleep. Whether you meet someone named Emmanuel or not, remember that Jesus Himself is Emmanuel, and He stays with you every minute of every day.

You are never alone. God is beside you, guiding, protecting, and helping you every single day.

LESSON / REFLECTION:
I am never alone. God is with me everywhere I go.

PRAYER:
Dear Jesus, thank You for being Emmanuel; God with us. Thank You for always being near and never leaving me alone. Help me to remember that You are with me in happy times and sad times. Amen.

ACTIVITY / THOUGHT FOR THE WEEK:
Write or draw some places you go during the week school, home, park, church. Next to each one, write: "God is with me here." Look at it every day and remember that Emmanuel is always with you.

> **VERSE TO REMEMBER:**
> *A child will be born to us. God will give a son to us. He will be responsible for leading the people. His name will be Wonderful Counselor, Powerful God, Father Who Lives Forever, Prince of Peace. — Isaiah 9:6.*

_____
_____
_____
_____
_____

MY YEAR WITH GOD
BIBLE VERSE: (REVIEW AND GOAL SETTING)

Teach us how short our lives really are. So that we may be wise." – Psalm 90:12.

DEVOTIONAL THOUGHT:
The end of the year is a special time to sit quietly and thank God for everything He helped you do. It is also the time to think about what you can do better in the new year because God loves it when we plan and grow with Him.

This week, spend some time with your parent, guardian, or leader in church to talk about your year.

Think and talk about these areas:
- Friendships: Was I kind and forgiving? Did I choose good friends?
- Schoolwork: Did I pay attention, study, and do my homework well?
- Family: Did I obey, help, and show love at home?
- Health: Did I eat well, rest, and take care of my body?
- My walk with God: Did I pray, read my Bible, and obey His Word?
- Activities and gifts: Did I use the special abilities God gave me to help others and glorify Him?

Now thank God for all the good things that happened. Make sure to put into writing the: very good, good, and not so good areas.

Don't feel sad about the not so good areas, talk to God about them and ask for His help to do better next time.

Setting Goals for the New Year:
God wants you to make plans, but He also wants to be part of them.
The Bible says, "Depend on the Lord in whatever you do. Then your plans will succeed." Proverbs 16:3. In setting goals for the coming year, use the report of this year as building blocks for the coming year: look at the things you did well, how you did them, the ones that did not go so well and how you did them.

Likely goals to add for the coming year:
- Praying every morning before school.
- Reading your Bible every day.
- Paying more attention in class and studying without being reminded.
- Drinking more water and eating fewer sugary or junk snacks.
- Helping more with chores at home.
- Being kinder and more patient with family and friends.
- Learning something new that you can use to serve God and make the world better.

You must write your goals and talk to God about them often. When you plan with God, your year becomes full of purpose and joy!

LESSON / REFLECTION:
I will think about how I spent my year, thank God for it, and plan the new one with Him by my side.

PRAYER:
Dear Father, thank You for being with me this year. Thank You for helping me grow and learn. As I plan for the new year, show me what You want me to do.

Give me wisdom to make good choices and the strength to reach my goals. In Jesus name I ask, Amen.

ACTIVITY / THOUGHT FOR THE WEEK:
Sit with a grown-up to review your year and set your new year goals.
Choose at least four goals: one about your faith, one about your family and friends, one about school, and one about your personal growth.
Keep your goals where you can see them and pray over them every week.

> **VERSE TO REMEMBER:**
>
> *"Depend on the Lord. Trust Him, and He will take care of you." – Psalm 37:5*

BIRTHDAY DEVOTIONAL
(GOD MADE THIS DAY SPECIAL FOR YOU)

BIBLE VERSE:

"You saw my body as it was formed. All the days planned for me were written in your book before I was one day old." — Psalm 139:16.

DEVOTIONAL THOUGHT:

Happy Birthday! Today is a very special day because it is the day God chose for you to enter the world. Before you were born, God already knew your name, your smile, your voice, your gifts, and every wonderful thing you would grow up to do. He planned every single one of your days - including this one.

Birthdays are not only about cake, balloons, and gifts. They are also a time to thank God for helping you grow, keeping you safe, teaching you, and loving you every day. When you think about the past year, remember all the ways God has been kind to you: at home, in school, in church, and with your friends.

Today is also the beginning of a brand-new year of your life. God has good plans for you. He wants you to grow in wisdom, kindness, strength, and faith. **And Jesus grew in wisdom and stature, and in favor with God and man. Luke 2:52 NIV**. You too are growing into the beautiful person God made you to be.

On your birthday, do something important:

Go to your parent or guardian and ask them to pray over you today; this is your special day.

And when next you see your pastor, ask him or her to speak a blessing over you.

Blessings are powerful, and God loves it when His children are blessed.

And as part of celebrating your new age, speak these words over yourself:

God will fulfil the number of my days; I will live long in Jesus' name.
My body is forever strong, and my mind is sound in Jesus' name.
I have all that I need in life in Jesus' name.
I am loved and accepted by all in Jesus' name.
I will grow and do great things in Jesus' name.

God is excited about your future, and He will walk with you every day of this new year of your life.

And I pray for you, your ways will be like the light of dawn, growing brighter and brighter daily, you will get better in all areas of your life daily in Jesus' name. Amen.

PRAYER:
Dear heavenly Father, thank You for giving me another year of life. Thank You for watching over me and helping me grow. Please bless my new year. Help me learn, love, obey, and shine for You. Fill my new age with joy, wisdom, protection, and Your presence. In Jesus name I ask, Amen.

ACTIVITY / THOUGHT FOR THE WEEK:
With the help of an adult, write three things you are thankful for from the past year. Then write three new things you want to grow in during your new age: it could be kindness, schoolwork, prayer, confidence, or anything God puts in your heart.

VERSE TO REMEMBER:

If you live wisely, you will live a long lime. Wisdom will add years to your life. — Proverbs 9:11.

WHEN I FEEL SICK
BIBLE VERSE:

"I will bring back your health. And I will heal your injuries," says the Lord. — Jeremiah 30:17a.

"You must worship the Lord your God. If you do, I will bless your bread and your water. I will take away sickness from you." — Exodus 23:25.

DEVOTIONAL THOUGHT:
Sometimes your body may feel weak: maybe you have a cold, a headache, a sore tummy, or your whole body just feels tired or painful. Feeling sick can make you sad or worried, and that's okay. Even adults feel like that too.

But here is something wonderful: God wants you to be well, He wants His children to be very well: He cares when you feel sick, and He stays close to you the whole time. Jesus healed many people in the Bible because He cared for them, and He cares about you just as much.

The Bible says that because you worship God, He will bless your food and your water, turning them into healing potions for your body every time you eat and drink. God Himself promises, "I will take away sickness from you." So anytime you are about to eat or drink; remember it is not just food or drinks before you, but nourishment and healing medicine.

In Matthew 15, Jesus talked about healing as the children's bread in God's kingdom.

That means healing belongs to you as God's child, just like the snacks in your house that your parents keep for you. When you feel sick, healing is already your right in Jesus.

When you don't feel well, tell your parent or guardian. They should help you rest, give you medicine, or take you to the doctor. God uses doctors and medicine to help your body get stronger, and He also listens when you pray. You can say: "Jesus, please make my body strong. Heal me and help me get better."

Even while you sleep or rest, God is working inside you, helping your body recover. And you do not have to be afraid; Jesus is with you.

LESSON / REFLECTION:
God wants to heal me.
Healing belongs to me because I am God's child.
God blesses my food and drinks and uses them to make my body strong.
I should tell my parent/guardian when I don't feel well.
God uses medicines and doctors to help me too.
I do not need to be afraid — Jesus is with me.

PRAYER:
Dear Jesus, thank You for loving me and staying close to me when I feel sick. Thank you because You want to heal me. Please heal my body and make me strong again. Bless my food and drinks and turn them into healing for my body. Help me not to be afraid and help everyone caring for me. Thank You because healing belongs to me in Your kingdom. Amen.

DECLARATIONS:
Healing belongs to me because I am God's child.
My food and drinks bring strength to my body.
My body is strong in Jesus' name.
God bless the medicines and make them work correctly in my body.
My carers know how to help me, because Jesus is helping them.

ACTIVITY / THOUGHT FOR THE WEEK:

When you feel unwell:
Ask an adult to pray for you.

Rest, drink water, and take your medicine if given.
In your mind, imagine a picture of Jesus holding your hand and helping you get better.

Say your healing declaration softly until you fall asleep.

VERSE TO REMEMBER:

The Lord forgives me for all my sins. He heals all my diseases. Psalms 103:3.

BAD DREAMS: PRAYERS FOR PEACEFUL SLEEP

BIBLE VERSE:

"I go to bed and sleep in peace. Lord, only You keep me safe." – Psalm 4:8.

DEVOTIONAL THOUGHT:

Sometimes you might have a bad dream or feel scared at night. Maybe you saw something that made you afraid, or your room feels too quiet or dark. But you don't have to be afraid because God is always with you, even while you sleep.

The Bible says that God never sleeps or rests (Psalms 121:4). That means while your eyes are closed, God's eyes are open, watching over you; you also have angels in heaven before God – "See that you don't despise any of these little ones. Their angels in heaven, I tell you, are always in the presence of my Father in heaven". – Matthew 18:10. When you pray before bedtime, you are inviting God to fill your room with His peace and His angels to protect you.

Ms Debola, what if the bad dream keeps coming?

Each time you wake up from a scary dream, remember the following:

1. You are not alone; Jesus is right there with you.
2. Jesus has given you the power to allow or not allow things, if you do not want bad dreams, you can reject them. **"I tell you the truth. The things you don't allow on earth will be the things God does not allow. The things you allow on earth will be the things that God allows." – Matthew 18:18.**
3. Immediately you wake up feeling scared or had a bad dream, you pray like this; **I chase out every scary presence and stop all bad dreams in Jesus' name**.

LESSON / REFLECTION:
I will not be afraid at night because God watches over me and gives me peaceful sleep.

PRAYER:
Dear Jesus, thank You for watching over me. Please take away every bad dream or fear from my heart. Let Your angels surround me and fill my room with peace. Help me to wake up rested and happy every morning. In Jesus name I ask, Amen.

ACTIVITY / THOUGHT FOR THE WEEK:
Before you sleep every day, read a Bible verse, sing a worship song, pray like this: Lord Jesus, anoint my heart, my room, our home with your presence.

My dreams are a holy ground, full of Jesus' light, there is no room for darkness in my dreams in Jesus' name, Amen.

VERSE TO REMEMBER:

"I can lie down and go to sleep. And I will wake up again because the Lord protects me." – Psalm 3:5.

_____

_____

_____

BACK TO SCHOOL: SHINE FOR JESUS
BIBLE VERSE:

"You are the light that gives light to the world. A city that is built on a hill cannot be hidden." – Matthew 5:14.

DEVOTIONAL THOUGHT:
A new school year means new teachers, new lessons, and maybe even new friends. It's exciting but it can also feel a little scary. The most important part? School is one of the places where you shine for Jesus the most.

Ms Debola, what does it mean to shine for Jesus?

It means letting your actions, attitude and hard work show that you belong to Jesus. Being diligent and hardworking is shining for Jesus, it makes Jesus smile and proud. Jesus loves and rewards hard workers; in Matthew 25:14-30, Jesus told a story about a master who, before traveling, told his servants to take care of his things while he was gone. He decided how much each servant would be able to care for and gave to them according to that. The ones who worked hard and excellently made their master happy and proud that he rewarded them. "His master answered, 'You did well. You are a good servant who can be trusted. You did well with small things. I will let you care for much greater things. Come and share my happiness with me.'" – Matthew 25:21.

Jesus wants you to be like those servants by using your mind, skills and time well. Consider your academics as one of the small things Jesus wants you to care for now, if you work hard and excellently, Jesus will trust you with bigger and better things.

Four ways to shine for Jesus in school:
1. Make learning your priority; God gave you a wonderful brain, use it very well, the more you use it, the better it gets.
2. No disruptive behaviour: don't shout, play or joke when you should be learning. – Ecclesiastes 3:1.
3. Respect teachers and school staff: your teachers, cleaners, cooks, security staff and every adult in school are elders. The bible teaches us to respect and honour those older than us. – Leviticus 19:32, 1Peter 5:5.
4. Obey school rules **(if they do not go against God's word):** rules help everyone stay safe and learn well. When you obey, you show good character and make Jesus proud.

LESSON / REFLCTION:
When I work hard, respect others, obey instructions, I am shining for Jesus!

PRAYER:
Dear Jesus, help me to shine for You in school. Help me to work hard, listen well, respect my teachers, and obey rules. Give me wisdom to learn well and strength to always do my best, make me a diligent and excellent student who makes You proud. In Jesus name I ask, Amen.

ACTIVITY / THOUGHT FOR THE WEEK:
Sit down and think about how you did in the last school year. With the help of an adult, write the areas where you did well; talk about them and write how to keep doing even better. Then write the areas where you struggled, and write simple steps you can take to improve this year.

VERSE TO REMEMBER:

"In the same way, you should be a light for other people. Live so that they will see the good things you do. Live so that they will praise your father in heaven." – Matthew 5:16.

CLOSING NOTE

Thank you for allowing this devotional to be part of your journey. My prayer is that everything you've learnt reveals God to you more deeply than before and inspires growth in every area of your life.

May your home be full of light, wisdom, and grace as you apply these teachings daily. Keep growing, keep shining, and keep walking in all that God has called you to be.

Warmly,
Ms Debola.

CONTACT THE AUTHOR

Thank you for going through Growing in Stature. If you have feedback, testimonies, questions, or would like to reach out for collaborations, please contact:

Email: adebolaadeoluwa@outlook.com

Instagram: @the.msdebola

Your feedback supports the continuous creation of wholesome, inspiring, and impactful resources that reach hearts, shape minds, and empower lives.

www.ingramcontent.com/pod-product-compliance
Lightning Source LLC
Chambersburg PA
CBHW080604170426
43196CB00017B/2899